FLIRTATION OR FACEOFF

D.C. EAGLES HOCKEY
BOOK 2

LEAH BRUNNER

EDITED BY
EJL EDITING

ILLUSTRATED BY
MELODY JEFFRIES

LEAH BRUNNER

TRIGGER WARNINGS

This work of fiction contains mild language and references to alcohol.

This book contains themes of parental divorce, and unfaithful exes.

To all the bookworms searching for their Aragorn:
I hope you find him.

COLBY
ONE YEAR AGO

WALKING up the steps toward the large front porch of my friend's—and teammate—new lakeside Minnesota cabin, I glance around, admiring the place. I'm flanked by two of our other teammates and note how huge the wrap-around front porch is, with plenty of space for three large, professional hockey players. Not an easy feat.

"This place is nice!" I say to Bruce and Remy.

Ford Remington, the team captain of the D.C. Eagles, but just Remy to me and the other guys on the team, nods his head in agreement. His close-cropped dark hair barely budging in the evening breeze.

My other teammate—and the best goalie in the NHL, in my opinion—Bruce McBride, grins and dances along to the music we can hear coming from inside the house. Unlike our captain, his hair is blond and messy. Blowing around his perpetually rosy cheeks with each burst of night air.

My phone pings with a text and I pull it out of my jeans pocket to read it.

UNKNOWN

> Hey Colby! This is Laci. Want to meet up later?

I hum to myself as I type out a response to the gorgeous redhead I sat next to on the flight here. And here I was worried Minnesota would be boring.

COLBY

> Yeah, what hotel are you staying at? We could grab drinks. *wink emoji*

LACI

> Drinks would be great. *wink emoji*

This is honestly too easy. Women don't even make it a challenge for me.

When I look up from my phone, Bruce and Remy are staring at me. Bruce is giving me a *you're the man* look, whereas Remy just appears irritated. I grin apologetically, then step forward and tug on the doorknob.

Remy nudges me with his elbow... hard, and I jerk my hand away from the door.

"Ow! What was that for?"

Bruce chuckles from my other side. "I think that's Remy's way of telling you to ring the doorbell instead of barging in."

"Were you raised by wolves, Knight?" Remy asks me, his arms now crossed over his chest. He's peering down his nose at me in a fatherly kind of way.

I want to remind him that I was raised by my strict, Italian mother, but instead, I throw my hands up dramatically. "Sheesh. West texted that she said yes to his proposal and that we can all join the celebration now."

We hear laughter from the other side of the door, making it

obvious that the party is going on without us. I raise my brows and gesture toward the sounds coming from inside the house. "See?"

Remy ignores me, steps forward, rings the doorbell, then falls back in line to wait with me and Bruce. If the music and noise are any indication, no one can even hear the doorbell. Slowly, I swivel my head to level an annoyed glance at Remy.

He groans and rings the doorbell again. We wait another minute, and no one comes.

From the corner of my eye, I see Bruce's hand come up to scratch the back of his head. "Uh, cap'n. I don't think anyone's coming."

Remy settles his hands on his hips and stares at the door. "I feel weird barging into someone's home."

With a sigh, I lean forward and knock on the door as hard as I can. This time, the door flies open.

It's dark outside, and it takes a moment for my eyes to adjust to the bright light filtering through the doorway. But when they do, I think I've died and gone to heaven. There is a literal angel in front of me. Easily the most beautiful woman I've ever seen. And I'm a professional hockey player, so trust me, I've seen a lot of beautiful women. Her short hair curls around her delicate face in perfect, golden ringlets. And the light coming from behind her outlines her head, and figure, with an angelic glow.

I will remember this moment for the rest of my life. The first time I saw *her*. The moment I knew love at first sight was a real thing.

She smiles and I almost fall over. Those perfectly pouty lips spread over a set of flawless white teeth. Because I've seen my fair share of teeth knocked out in my career, they're something I always notice. If it wasn't for modern dentistry, I'd have several gaps in my smile. But I'm shallow and fixed them with dental implants. This face is my moneymaker.

Instantly, I forget anyone else is in our orbit. I wink at her and give her a wide grin… the one I've been told showcases my dimples.

"Hey, angel. Mind if we come in?"

One of her light brown eyebrows raises slightly. But it's enough to show me she has an attitude, this one.

Even better.

"Can you tell me who this cabin belongs to?" she asks, playing security guard in the sexiest way possible.

"Weston Kershaw and Melanie," I answer.

She leans against the door frame, her brown eyes not leaving mine. "And what's Mel's last name?"

I shrug. "Do you need their socials and birth dates too?"

That makes her laugh. She sloughs off the door jamb and steps out of the way to allow us entrance. Honestly, for such a twiggy woman, she makes an excellent bouncer.

I hold her gaze as I allow the other guys to walk into the house, and then slowly walk past her myself. I allow my eyes to blatantly dip down her body and she blushes fiercely. Feisty *and* shy? She's my dream woman.

I stop once I'm inside the house and standing right in front of her, jutting one hand out in front of her waist. "Colby Knight."

She reluctantly pushes her long, slender fingers into mine and shakes. "Noel Woodcock."

My saliva, probably accumulated from drooling over her, catches in my throat. "I'm sorry, Noel Wood… what?"

She straightens her spine and releases my hand. "I said," She clears her throat dramatically. "Noel Woodcock. Dr. Woodcock, please."

I choke again. "Dr. Woodcock…?"

Those amber eyes are deadly as she fixes me with a look that is both scathing and ridiculously sexy. "You're quite mature, I can tell." She turns on a heel and starts to walk away.

I follow her the way an eager puppy would, waiting for attention. "So, how do you know West and Mel?"

"I'm Mel's best friend, we met at college. And now we're roommates." She keeps walking as she speaks, not even sparing a glance at me over her angular shoulder.

Stopping abruptly, she turns toward me... causing her chest to bump into mine. She's tall, not nearly as tall as me. But taller than most women. The perfect height to kiss without having to crane my neck too much.

She studies me, holding my gaze intensely. "How do *you* know West and Mel?"

I grin. "I'm West's teammate."

Her face instantly falls. "You're a hockey player?"

"Yeah, angel. At your service." I dip my head in a bow.

"Oh," she says, looking me over and then turning away.

I stare after her, stupefied. What did I do wrong? Women have rarely rejected me... and I've certainly never gotten that reaction after admitting to being a pro athlete. Women usually eat that up.

But something tells me Noel—sorry, Dr. Woodcock—isn't a typical woman.

West's voice draws my attention from across the room. I peek over in the direction of his voice and find West beaming with one arm around his new-fiancée's waist. Bruce and Remy are beside them, Bruce is chatting animatedly, and Remy has a pleasant smile on his face. I assume they're congratulating the newly engaged couple. I realize I'm in the center of the open concept living, dining, and kitchen area and everyone is staring at me. But I was too focused on the blonde to even notice anyone else.

I take three giant steps past the dozen other people in the room, probably West and Mel's family members, toward the couple and pull them both into a bear hug. "Congratulations, you two!"

"Colby," Mel chokes out, her face somewhere in my armpit.

Unlike Noel, Mel is petite, minuscule, really. West towers over her, as do I. I pull away, allowing her room to breathe. "Sorry, Mel."

She laughs and West shoves me. "Stop trying to suffocate my wife."

"Dude, she's not even your wife yet."

Mel laughs and West drapes a protective arm across her shoulders. Something across the room catches her attention and she cups a hand around her mouth, yelling, "Noel! Come meet the guys!"

I crane my head to look at her. She's in the kitchen talking to West's mom. She hesitates before excusing herself and walking toward us. Her movements are graceful, they remind me of the elegant way figure skaters move. I used to watch them before hockey practices when I was a kid.

Noel gives me a tense smile when she stops in our circle, right between me and Mel. "Guys, this is my best friend, Noel," Mel introduces her friend before gesturing to Bruce. "This is Bruce, the Eagle's starting goalie, and an eighties music expert."

Bruce grins and holds his large hand out to shake hers. My shoulders tense as I watch him touch her, which surprises me. I'm not a jealous guy, or possessive. But something about seeing someone else's hand on hers makes my stomach coil.

Noel pumps his hand a few times and smiles. "I've heard so much about you!"

Remy is introduced next. "Remy is the team captain, and he keeps all of these guys out of trouble."

Remy nods, agreeing with her assessment, then gives Noel's hand a quick squeeze. Not quite a high five, but not a full handshake.

I'll allow it.

"And this is Colby!" Mel winks at me. "Don't let his mischievous smile fool you—this guy would drop everything for a friend in need."

I'm touched by her words, and that she knows me this well in such a short time. Women never usually get past my face, or my income. Feeling oddly uncomfortable at my proverbial mask being briefly removed, I laugh off her comment and drape an arm around Noel's shoulders.

"Hey, angel. We must stop meeting like this."

She shoves out of my grasp with a roll of her eyes. When she turns her attention toward Bruce and Remy, she gives them a friendly, megawatt smile. "It's nice officially meeting you guys!" She side-eyes me. "*Most* of you."

What does a guy have to do to get one of those megawatt smiles aimed at him?

While Noel's focus is on my teammates, I take the opportunity to check her out properly. I was hyper focused on her height and face earlier; and I'm realizing I wasn't getting the full effect. She's barefoot, which surprises me. I'm used to women wearing heels, and still being ten inches shorter than I am. Noel is wearing high-waisted denim shorts with gold buttons on the front, giving her the appearance of being a sexy sailor. A navy and white striped top is tucked into the little shorts, completing the simple yet classy summer outfit. My eyes dip down to her impossibly long, lean legs and I stare a few seconds too long and hear the clearing of a throat. My eyes snap up to see Dr. Woodcock herself glaring at me with her arms crossed.

Damn, I might've stuck it out in college a little longer if I'd have had a professor as stunning as this woman—and had I not been signed by the Eagles junior year.

My lips tug upward in a smirk, hopefully hiding my confusion. Noel is completely different from my usual type. I can't help but wonder what it is about her that demands my attention—aside from the sexy as hell Gilligan's Island thing she's got going on with this outfit.

Her hair is short, probably shorter than Bruce's, which shows off her long, elegant neck. The blonde bob is curly too, giving her an innocent quality. Her eyes are a light, golden brown. The color of honey… and halos.

Noel comes across innocent, intelligent, refined… yet she has a down-to-earth quality, too. She gives me the impression that you could take her to a Michelin star restaurant, *or* rollerblading, and she'd be down either way.

My attraction to her is a mystery. I'm probably drawn to the fact that she's a challenge. I'm not used to having to pursue anyone, they always do the work for me. But not Noel.

Melanie and West's families join our group, squeezing their way between me and Noel. West disappears for a moment and returns with personalized red hockey jerseys for all of us. They say *Wesanie* on the back, West and Melanie's couple name.

We all slip our jerseys on as a delivery guy drops off a bunch of pizzas. We eat as West and Mel's families share stories of the two growing up. I wonder what it would be like to marry your childhood crush. Mel's brother, Harrison, who also happens to be West's best friend, appears stiff and uncomfortable when West kisses his little sister a million times throughout the evening. Having a little sister myself, I'm sure I'll be the same way when she grows up. But I can't help but laugh under my breath.

I try to ignore Noel. She's way too angelic for me. But my eyes can't stop tracking her every move. And my body is hyper aware of her presence. When she leaves the room, I know. When she stands, I know. When she yawns, stretching her arms up over her head the way a sleepy cat would... I know. Since when does watching a girl yawn make me want to kiss her? Or take her sleepy form into my arms and put her to bed.

I shake my head, willing the thoughts away. *It's just a crush, Colby. You'll get over it in an hour or less*, I tell myself.

But I never met Laci for drinks that night.

CHAPTER 1
COLBY
THREE MONTHS AGO

IT'S West's bachelor party. Our boy wanted low-key, and that's what he got. Only because he chose his childhood best friend, Harrison, as his best man instead of me.

We're all floating around in tubes. West and Mel are getting hitched at their lakefront property in Minnesota, but us guys get the cabin to ourselves tonight. We all have beer cans in hand, except Mitch, the Eagle's top defenseman. He doesn't drink and he's clutching a bottle of water. Country music is playing from the surround sound speakers West installed soon after purchasing this place last year.

This is for sure the most wholesome bachelor party I've ever taken part in. I won't lie, it's refreshing. West has no desire to have one last night of partying before tying himself to someone forever. He doesn't see it that way. He can't wait to marry Mel, she's his everything. He has no interest in dancing with other women, or to have women shaking around in front of him.

It's the real deal, what they have. Something I didn't think was possible until I saw Ma fall in love and re-marry last year, and then watching West and Mel's relationship unfold.

Mitch's tube floats over and bumps into mine. I reach my arm out and tap my beer against his water bottle. "Still can't believe you're one of West's groomsmen," I say, remembering how they hated each other all of last year.

"You and me both." He scoffs, then checks his wristwatch. "Is it really necessary for me to stay overnight?" he whispers. "Are we eight years old?"

"Bachelor parties are usually an all-night thing, Mitch."

Bruce overhears me and uses his arms to paddle his tube closer to us. "Man, it's been forever since I went to a slumber party! We should do this more often."

Remy is several yards away from us and makes no move to come closer. Instead, he rolls his eyes.

West flops onto his belly on his tube and uses his legs to kick himself nearer. He holds his beer high, so it doesn't get any lake water in it. "It's not a slumber party! We're *men*!"

Bruce puffs his chest out and makes his voice even deeper. "Sorry, a manly slumber party."

We all laugh, even the perpetually-grumpy Mitch cracks a smile.

West pounds his fists against his chest the way Tarzan would. "That's right! Now what time is the pillow fight again?"

Harrison, whose tube is close to Remy's, sends West an unamused glance. "There's no pillow fight, West."

Bruce chuckles. "You can have a pillow fight tomorrow night, West." He winks in an overexaggerated way, with his mouth open.

"Oh yeah!" I grin. "Maybe even in your underwear, if you're lucky."

Bruce waggles his eyebrows. "Or without underwear."

Harrison chokes on the sip of beer he just swallowed. He

pounds his fist against his sternum a few times. "Stop! That's my sister!"

Bruce cringes. "Oh yeah, I forgot. Sorry, man."

Mitch groans, paddling away from us toward Harrison and Remy. Obviously, he's too manly and serious to be with us right now.

"You old men enjoy your quiet time; the party is over here though," I yell so they can hear me, and I'm met with unamused stares.

"We're playing NHL on the Xbox all night, right?" West asks, sounding a little too excited at the prospect of a video game.

"Oh." I stick my bottom lip out in a childish pout. "I'm not sure. Harrison is your best man; you'll have to ask him."

West snorts a laugh, reaching over and mussing my damp lake hair. "You're such a big baby. Keep it up and I'll switch your job from groomsman to flower boy."

I lift my chin in challenge. "I'd be an excellent flower boy and you know it."

Bruce and West laugh, and my fake pout melts into laughter as well. "So, what are the bridesmaids wearing tomorrow?" I ask, trying to picture how Noel might look. I've been around her several times since meeting her last year, since she's never too far from Mel. But despite all my best flirting, she still acts disgusted by me.

West glances up at the sky, now fading into twilight. "Honestly, I'm not sure. I know the colors are seafoam green and coral."

"What the hell is seafoam green?" Bruce's face twists in disgust. "I'm imagining a puke green."

West snorts a laugh. "No clue. I only cared about Mel being at the end of that aisle walking toward me. The rest was all her. And she lives for this event planning, organization stuff. I'm sitting back and letting her do her thing."

"Smart man," Harrison's voice says over my shoulder. He's floated our way and stops when his tube hits mine. I take him in quickly, dark hair, brown eyes, long limbs. Basically, the opposite of his sister in every way. Except for the pointed chin and round puppy dog eyes.

"You're a physical therapist, right?" I blurt, causing his head to whip in my direction.

"Yeah, I love it." He smiles wistfully.

"You should work for the Eagles. We can always use good physical therapists."

"West has told me the same thing. Maybe when I have nieces and nephews to spoil, I'll want to be closer." He gives West a pointed stare.

West throws his head back in a laugh. "Let us get through the wedding first."

I laugh. "Hurry up with that, West. I want to hang out with Harrison more."

Bruce shoves my tube. "Dude, maybe he lives in a different city because he doesn't want to see his little sister making out with his best friend."

Harrison cringes, but his shoulders relax in relief, like Bruce gave him the perfect excuse. "Yeah, exactly. Bruce gets it."

West chuckles. "Sorry, not sorry," he teases, tipping his beer can into his mouth and finishing it. "Alright guys, I'm starving."

Harrison's eyes flick down to his watch. "Perfect, because the delivery guy just dropped off our Chipotle order."

All the guys, even Mitch and Remy, start paddling toward the dock as fast as they can.

The following morning, we're all dapper as hell in our wedding attire. All the groomsmen are wearing navy blue slacks with leather oxfords, and white button-down shirts with seafoam green ties. It's a formal but casual look, fitting for a lakeside wedding.

We're in the large guest room downstairs, leaving the master bedroom to the girls. There's only one floor-length mirror and Bruce is hogging it. He studies his tie in the mirror, touching it carefully.

"So, this is seafoam green." His mouth quirks in approval as he nods. "Much better than I expected."

West shoves him out of the way, sweeping a hand over his normally shaggy, blond hair, which is currently gelled to perfection. "My girl would never choose puke green. She's got impeccable taste." He puffs his chest out to add emphasis to his point.

West's father bursts into the room. His eyes, grey-blue like West's, instantly fill with tears at the sight of his son getting ready to marry his dream girl.

"Wow. You're so handsome, son! Mom and the girls wanna know if they can come in. Everybody decent?"

West chuckles. "Yep, everyone's dressed."

His mom and sisters file into the room and they all embrace West in a big group hug. I glance over at Remy, Bruce and Mitch, who look stiff and uncomfortable. I think we all feel like we're intruding upon a private family moment. Clearing my throat quietly to get their attention, I raise my chin toward the door, and we subtly leave the room.

Once we're in the quiet hallway, Remy exhales a sigh of relief. "Wow, that was emotional."

Mitch slumps against the wall. "Ugh, is this whole day going to be emotional?"

"It's a wedding," I whisper.

Mitch shrugs. "So what? No one better cry at my wedding." He shivers like the idea is horrible.

Bruce snorts quietly. "You'll be the one crying at your wedding. Just watch."

Mitch glares at him, causing Remy and I to snicker.

Bruce digs in the pockets of his pants and pulls out a can of shaving cream and a box of condoms. "Who wants to help me decorate West's car?"

Mitch and Remy snicker, clearly on board with the idea.

I wave a hand. "You guys go on without me. I'm going to go see if the girls need anything," I say, going for a nonchalant tone.

They all study me with quirked brows, seeing right through me. But they don't say anything, and head toward the garage door in search of West's car.

I turn, walking around the corner toward the kitchen. As soon as I round the corner, a feminine body slams into me. I steady her by gently grabbing her arms with my hands, then I realize it's Noel simply from the vanilla, sugar-cookie scent overwhelming my senses.

Wow, she makes me want a cookie so bad.

"Oh, I'm sorry!" She grabs my forearms, a knee jerk reaction so she doesn't stumble again. She peers up at my face, registering who's holding her for the first time and her cheeks instantly flame. She's caught off guard, and I wonder if this is the first genuine reaction I've seen from her. Perhaps, she's not so unaffected by me, after all.

My mouth pulls up in a slow, satisfied grin. "That's alright, angel. You okay?"

She pushes away from me and takes a few steps back. "I'm fine."

The distance allows me to get my first glimpse of her in her bridesmaid dress. I have to close my gaping mouth to keep my drool from dripping onto the floor. Hot damn, this woman. Her dress is a pinkish red color and fitted perfectly on top, with one thin strap going around the back of her neck. The bodice shows off her slim figure, then the delicate fabric flows out at her waist, giving the dress a fun and youthful flare. Coral is a great color on her, enhancing her fair complexion. I love that I can see her smooth skin and that it's not marred by a spray tan. The urge to pull her back in my arms and place a kiss on one of those bare shoulders nearly steals my breath away.

I blink a few times, trying to get the Noel-induced-haze from my eyes. "You look—" I'm at a loss for words.

"Like a bridesmaid?" She pinches her lips to the side; she seems unsure, maybe even self-conscious. Another look into the real woman.

"Breathtaking."

Her eyes widen in surprise, probably because I gave her a genuine compliment. No obnoxious, over-the-top flirting. Just stating the first thought that popped into my head. Her eyes drop down to my feet and then quickly back up to my face.

"You look nice, too." Her voice is strained, like it literally pains her to pay me a compliment.

"Thank you."

We stare at each other for a moment, neither of us knowing what to say next. We've never had a real, non-sarcastic conversation before.

She blinks a few times, then brushes past me into the spacious kitchen. Noel starts taking items out of the fridge and setting them on the marble countertop.

"What are you doing?" I ask, striding into the kitchen and leaning against the marble countertop.

Her back is toward me as she digs in the fridge. "The bride needs lunch. And as the maid of honor, I'm making sure she gets exactly what she wants today."

She bends at the waist to take something off one of the lower shelves. I notice the way the skirt of her dress hikes up, exposing more of those long, lean thighs. I squeeze my eyes shut and count backward from ten, trying to get the image out of my mind.

"Why are you making that face?" Noel's voice draws me back to the present and I open my eyes.

"Uh, nothing. I'll help you make lunch."

She sighs, then turns and opens a cabinet. The plates are on the top shelf, and she stretches to grab them. "I don't need your help."

Noel is a few inches too short to reach the plates. This is my time to shine. I settle right behind her, placing a hand on her waist so I don't startle her. Reaching up, I easily grab the plates off the shelf with my other hand. When I step back, I set them on the counter next to the other supplies she's accumulated.

Her face and chest are pink with a delicious blush, and I have to fight a smile. I decide that although Noel doesn't *want* to be attracted to me, she definitely is. Now my curiosity is piqued... if she's attracted to me, why does she fight it?

Clearing her throat, Noel schools her face back into a neutral expression. She begins opening up a bunch of containers filled with absurdly healthy-looking food and assembling a salad.

"Are those seeds?" I ask, eyeing one that appears to be tiny, brown dots.

"It's quinoa."

"And that?" I point to a container full of green liquid.

"Homemade dressing."

"And what about that?" I nudge a container filled with chopped lettuce, just to be annoying, and hoping she'll finally look at me.

She groans. "That's lettuce, Colby." Her eyes meet mine and she purses her lips.

"Oh!" I grin. "Do you always eat this healthy?"

"It's not for me. Mel eats a special diet for her anxiety." The dressing spills as she spoons it over the top of the salad she's compiled.

Stepping toward the sink, I grab a few paper towels and hand them to her. She grabs them quickly and her fingers brush mine. Those honey eyes meet mine for a split second and she inhales a sharp breath before turning away from me quickly and wiping up the mess.

I take in her formal dress and heels, and it strikes me how out of place she looks here in the kitchen. Surely there's someone else who can prep lunch? Shouldn't Noel be upstairs with the other girls taking photos and fussing over their eyeliner, or whatever the hell women do. "Why didn't you order food from town?"

"You ask a lot of questions."

I stay silent, waiting for an answer.

"The nearest town didn't have anything that was gluten and dairy free. So, I stayed up late making this. Mel didn't want me to fuss over her, and she doesn't know this isn't from a restaurant. And she *won't* find out." She stares me down to get her point across.

My entire face softens at her words. One more thing to admire about Noel: she puts others first and takes care of those she loves. Add this to her intelligence and gracefulness and it's almost unbearable how perfect she is.

She sinks down on her haunches and rummages through a

lower cabinet before popping back up with a takeout container she must've stashed at some point. It still has a sticker on it from the café she got it from, but it's obviously been washed. Noel dumps the salad she made into the container and pops the lid on.

She then heads toward the stairs but turns back to look at me, motioning with her hand like she's zipping her mouth shut, then points at me. A plea to keep her secret.

I nod and make a cross over my heart.

I would keep all of her secrets, if she'd let me.

CHAPTER 2
NOEL
PRESENT DAY

"AND THAT WAS the downfall of the Roman empire," I finish my lecture with a bang, as usual. Have to keep the students' interests piqued. Although half of them appear to be bored out of their minds. Two of the students here on hockey scholarship are asleep in the back row.

I'll never understand people who aren't enthralled by history. Everything in our modern world was inspired or affected by history.

Even the lecture hall my class takes place in is a reminder of the Roman Colosseum. I'm down at the bottom, and the seats for the students rise above me. Thankfully, I'm simply giving a lecture, and showing slides on the screen, instead of wielding giant swords like the guy in The Gladiator.

When class ends, the students filter out of the room. Some stop and smile, others ignore me completely, and a few linger to flirt with me, thinking they're being charming. The boys here on hockey scholarship are awake now and ask me to extend the deadline for their mid-term papers. They claim the deadline I made is impossible with their hockey schedule. They even go so far as to brace their hands in their armpits, as if trying to make their biceps appear bigger. Like that's going to convince me to help them out.

If only they worked as hard in history class as they do in the gym.

I give them a tight, professional smile. "The deadline is nonnegotiable, *boys*. But there is a study group that meets in the library if you need some extra help." I turn and grab a flier from my desk that has the information for the study group on it, and hand it to the dark-haired one. "Have a good weekend." They leave with a groan, not bothering to tell me to have a good weekend too.

All athletes are the same: egotistical, unfaithful, narcissistic, and *will* break your heart... guaranteed. Which is one of the reasons why I swore off athletes a decade ago.

My best friend's husband, Weston Kershaw, is the exception. But West and my bestie, Mel, have known each other since childhood, and he didn't let fame and money get to his head.

The alarm goes off on my phone and I grab my satchel from behind the large desk. Tapping the screen to turn off the alarm, I pack up my things for my meeting with the dean of the history department.

Quickly, I make my way across the sprawling campus to the main building that houses the dean's offices. It's a gorgeous late-September day here in Arlington, Virginia. Warm enough not to need a coat, but cool enough for long sleeves. I enjoy watching the colorful leaves falling from the ancient trees around campus, the fall colors made all the more vibrant by the lovely brick buildings surrounding me. A cool breeze rushes past me, making my bare neck prickle. I shiver slightly and wrap my arms around myself. Only when it's chilly outside do I ever consider growing my hair longer. But these curls are a mess, and I know it would drive me nuts if it was longer.

I enter Arlington University's main building, my heels clacking against the antique tiles as I walk. When I reach the office that belongs to the dean of the history department, I knock lightly on the lacquered, oak door.

"Come in," her voice rings from the other side of the door.

With a smile, I let myself into the familiar space. Dean Morris is typing something on her computer but glances up as I close the door behind me. Her lips tug upward, and she removes her silver glasses. Dean Morris has black hair, freckled with grey, pulled into a sleek chignon at the back of her head. Her kind brown eyes always twinkle in a way that makes you wonder if she knows something everyone else doesn't. Perhaps, that's why she wears a permanent smirk. She's intimidating when she needs to be, but normally, she's the sweetest person.

"Dr. Woodcock, you look lovely as always."

My eyes flick down to my brown tweed trousers, leather suspenders, and white button-down shirt. One of my favorite outfits. I know my old-world style isn't for everyone, but I love mixing historical pieces with modern ones. And my black pointed-toe pumps give the ensemble the modern touch it needs.

"Thank you." I smile and take a seat in one of the hunter-green wingback chairs across from her polished-oak desk. "So, what did you need to see me about?" I get straight to the point, knowing I have another class in an hour and a half and still need to grab lunch.

She gives me her full attention, steepling her hands on her desk. "You know the D.C. Children's Hospital's charity gala Saturday?"

I nod.

"I was planning on attending it myself, but Mr. Morris planned a surprise getaway for us this weekend." Her eyes flit to the picture frame on her desk, one I know holds a photo of her and her husband. Still madly in love after thirty-plus years of marriage. "I hoped you might attend in my place. I know how you love an occasion to dress up." She winks.

I laugh. "I'd be honored. I'm already planning my outfit."

"I have two tickets; you should bring a date." Her eyebrows raise slightly.

I look up at the ceiling, pretending I'm deep in thought. "Oh wow, it's going to be difficult to choose. Do I ask Brad, Derek, or Chad? I have *so* many romantic interests in my current repertoire."

She chuckles. "I'm sure you'll figure it out. And I'll need you to bid on an item, the University has allotted twenty thousand dollars for the charity event. So, win something good for us."

"Will do."

"Perfect, I'll email you the tickets and all the details right away. Thanks for doing this for me." She grabs her glasses and places them back on her face. "I know you have places to be, and Brads, Chads and Dereks to see. I won't keep you any longer."

My head falls back in a laugh. "Alright," I stand. "You have fun with Mr. Morris this weekend."

We say our goodbyes, and I walk the short distance to the building next door which has a food court and a cute coffee shop inside.

Opening the door to the campus's coffee shop, I take a few steps inside and slam into the sweater-vest clad chest of Dexter Hawthorne. My work crush.

Meeting his dark eyes, my face heats. Forget the chill in the air I felt earlier, I'm plenty warm now, and from the warmth of my face, I assume also bright red. Ugh.

Dexter steadies me, reaching for my elbow with one of his long, slim arms. He smiles slightly, always in control of himself and never ruffled. I smile back, unable to think of words with him touching me.

He transferred here from a university in England last fall. He's handsome, educated, totally dreamy, *and* he has a British accent. I've done my best flirting—which honestly, isn't great —and he still doesn't pay attention to me. He's never even checked me out.

If I was braver, I'd ask him to the charity gala. But I'm not. And I want to *be* pursued... not the other way around. I'm a strong and independent woman, sure. But I'm also an old soul who loves anything written by the Brontë sisters.

Say what you will about Heathcliff, but Cathy never once doubted his love for her. Heathcliff knew how to pursue a woman. He probably could've stopped after Cathy married someone else, though.

"Um, are you okay, Dr. Woodcock?" His English accented voice drips with class.

I blink a few times, realizing I'm still staring. "Oh, yeah! Thank you, Dr. Heathcliff." My eyes nearly fall out of my head when I realize my mistake. "I mean, Dr. Hawthorne!"

He gives me a confused smile. "Alright, well, I must get to class now. Enjoy some coffee, maybe it will help you wake up."

"Ha, you too!" I say back as he exits the door, making the little bell ding. I realize he wasn't even holding coffee, and instantly feel like a moron.

Here I am, an intelligent, conventionally attractive woman, who loses her wits around a man I find handsome. All the historical feminists and women's rights icons I've studied would be rolling over in their graves.

I haven't dated anyone since the heartbreak I experienced with my college boyfriend. The only guys I meet are usually colleagues who are way older than me, or students, who are much younger.

I'm the personification of that quote from Charlotte Lucas in the 2005 adaptation of Pride and Prejudice. Except I'm twenty-nine years old... and I'm financially stable. I'm also probably not a burden to my parents... but I *am* frightened, and I certainly don't have any prospects.

"Ma'am... ma'am!"

I blink a few times, registering that the annoyed student behind the coffee counter is waiting for me to order.

"Oh! Sorry! I'll have a chai latte... with a spot of cream," I say with confidence. I wish Dexter was here to listen to my order, then he'd know I'm practically British too and we're a match made in heaven. But, alas, he only ever witnessed me fumbling around like an imbecile and making a fool of myself.

Is there a grad school for learning to be suave? That's the course I need. Maybe I can double major in flirting, since I'm also horrible at that.

Why can't guys be impressed by my knowledge of eighteenth-century literature?

CHAPTER 3
COLBY

SKATING as fast as I can toward Bruce, who's in net during practice, I beat out the rookies in our race from one end of the ice to the other. For a theatrical ending to my performance, I do a classic hockey stop in front of the net, spraying ice chips all over Bruce like a tiny blizzard.

He splutters, blinking rapidly to clear his face of the ice. "You asshole," he says, but he's laughing. "Still faster than the young pups, eh?"

"Of course." I straighten my spine, trying not to feel old since my thirtieth birthday is next week. I realize thirty isn't necessarily old, but in hockey, it's ancient. The rookies are eyeing me and moaning about me beating them in speed drills, so I don't think I have anything to worry about yet.

I glance over at Coach Young, who's studying the new guys and a defenseman they brought in from our minor league team and making notes on his iPad. This is our last week of training before the preseason officially begins. Us older, veteran players don't participate much in those games, but it's a good way for the coaches to see how the rookies do, and hopefully sign a few of them.

The new defenseman skates past me on his way to his water bottle on the bench. "Hey, man! Good work out there today. It's Travis, right?" I ask him.

I notice he's skating slowly and favoring his left leg over his right. "Yeah," he grunts, not bothering to smile or be friendly. Maybe it's because he pulled a muscle, or maybe he's simply a jerk. Time will tell.

"You okay?" I follow him to the bench.

"I'm fine." He grimaces, rubbing his leg through his pads. "Nothing an ice pack can't cure." He still doesn't smile or act like he wants to chat, so I leave him alone.

West skates up beside me, he's had a big grin on his face all during practice.

"You're a little slow today, West. Mel keep you up last night?"

He shoves me but still can't wipe the smile off his face. So, I'm guessing the answer is yes. I laugh and his face turns red. Which makes me laugh harder. "Don't be embarrassed, you're practically still on your honeymoon. Wear your exhaustion like a badge of honor."

Remy skates over but keeps his eyes on the new guys. Probably making notes about them internally, similar to coach. Being the team captain, I'm sure coach Young will want Remy's input.

"Wear what like a badge of honor?" Remy asks.

I swear, his hearing is unnervingly sharp. West gives me a serious glare, silently ordering me not to tell him what we were actually talking about.

Keeping it clean, I offer, "Being a married man, of course."

Remy's face swivels to focus on me and West. "I'm sure marriage is great, but you were awfully slow out there today, Kershaw." Remy's voice is so serious, it takes me a full five seconds to realize he's joking.

He winks at West then skates off, leaving me with my blushing teammate. I snicker and he shoves me over.

Mitch, our top defenseman, appears out of nowhere. He extends a hand and hoists me back up to my skates. He's smirking, which is new for him. Six months ago, I didn't think his face was capable of smiling or smirking... but then he met Andie, who's now his fiancée.

"Let's hope Kershaw isn't this distracted all season," he grumbles, but doesn't seem that annoyed.

"You're next, you know. Before we realize what's happening, the entire team is going to be a bunch of twitterpated newlyweds."

He snorts an undignified laugh. "My focus cannot be deterred. Not even by Andie." Suddenly, his attention goes somewhere over my left shoulder and his face contorts into a big smile. It's weird when he smiles, like he's using muscles he's never used before. It reminds me of a foal taking its first steps. I peer over my shoulder and see Andie and her little brother, Noah, behind the glass watching us practice.

"Laser focused, huh?"

He ignores me and skates over to greet them. Probably wishing he could kiss her through the plexiglass.

Shaking my head, I grab my water bottle from the bench and head over to the net to chat with Bruce. He's watching Mitch and Andie, who are beaming at each other like they've spent a year apart.

"Everyone's getting married, man. You gonna be next?" Bruce teases.

"I'd get married next week if Noel would ever say yes." I raise my eyebrows up and down.

He grabs his water bottle from the back of the net and squirts me with it. "I think you have to get her to agree to a date first."

I wave my hand in front of me nonchalantly. "Details."

Bruce huffs a laugh. "Honestly, I thought your infatuation with her would wear off by now."

"You and me both." I glance down at my skates, wondering for the millionth time why it *hasn't* gone away. I haven't even seen her since West and Mel's wedding in July, and still, she's the only woman on my mind.

After practice, I shower and change. When I start toward the parking lot to head home, a *pst* comes from Coach Young's office as I walk past.

"Knight, get in here," Coach Young demands.

I backtrack a few steps, walking backward inside his office moonwalk style. He sighs heavily and his eyes flick to one of the chairs inside the room near his desk.

Grabbing a chair, I scoot it closer to his desk and take a seat. Coach's office is nice but simple, there are jerseys and hockey memorabilia all over the walls and two windows allowing natural light in.

"Miss me already, Coach? It's only been... what? Thirty minutes?"

His eyes do something weird as if he's about to roll them but stops himself. Instead, he schools his features into a faint smile. "I need a favor."

My stomach does a weird flip. This can't be good. Coach Young, and our general manager, Tom Parker, always ask Remy for favors. The mature, steady Remy. Never me. I swallow. "Okay," I say, widening my eyes, urging him to continue.

"There's a charity gala this weekend."

I instantly relax. A gala, no big deal. I lean back in the chair and give him my signature Colby Knight grin. "Ahh, and you need a date. Why didn't you say so?" I wink at him.

"Knight," he says in a reprimanding tone. "Be serious for five seconds."

"Okay, fine. Continue."

"Well, Tom asked me months ago to arrange an *'evening with a D.C. Eagle'* for the charity auction. And I forgot about it until now." He nervously adjusts the collar of his navy blue polo. "Naturally, I need one of you to be the Eagle in the *evening with a D.C. Eagle.*"

My eyebrows shoot up. "You're auctioning one of us off?"

"Only for one evening! Dinner," he stutters. "And it's for a good cause! The auction will fund research for the children's hospital."

My shoulders slacken. The team has several community outreach opportunities for us, but volunteering at the children's hospital is my favorite. My mind is already made up, but I decide to mess with Coach some more. Enjoying how nervous he is. "Let me get this straight, I'm supposed to sell my body, a *very* nice body mind you, for children's research?"

"No, no, no." He stands from his seat and starts waving his hands around. "You've got this all wrong. Let me start over." Sweat forms on his brow.

I throw my head back and laugh. When I bring my head back up, I notice Coach Young is scowling at me.

"Will you do it or not?"

"Yeah, yeah." I nod. "I'll do it. What do I get out of it?"

"You'll get the satisfaction of knowing the auction money is helping children's research. And probably a lovely dinner out with a wealthy old man."

With a sigh, I push out of the chair and take a step toward the door. "I guess I can handle that." I turn to leave but stop in the doorway. "Why'd you ask me and not Remy or Bruce?"

"Remy said no. Emphatically." Coach slumps back down into his office chair. "Then he told me to ask you. Said you think you look like 007 in a tux."

I chuckle. "I don't think I do; I *know* I do."

He ignores my sarcasm. "Thanks for doing this, I'll text you the details." He waves a hand toward the door, letting me know I'm dismissed.

———

When I arrive home from practice, I open the door from my four-car garage that leads to a spacious mud room, then into the kitchen. Stepping inside, I toe my shoes off on the mat, not wanting to mess up my freshly cleaned tile floors. As I come into the kitchen, I spot the familiar brunette messy bun that my mother always puts her hair in. Ma worked hard cleaning houses to make it as a single mom. She made a lot of sacrifices for me to play hockey, it's not a cheap sport. When I got picked up by the Eagles, I moved her here with me. I've paid her to clean my place every week and cook my meals for me ever since. Cheaper than a chef, and Ma didn't lose her income. Plus, her Italian cooking is amazing… and the thought of her all alone in New York broke my heart.

I grin, coming up behind her and grabbing her shoulders. She nearly jumps out of her skin with a shriek. "Colby! How can such a large person be so quiet?"

I chuckle. "You've never accused me of being quiet before."

Her brown eyes twinkle. "True. You were always in trouble for talking in class. And nothing has changed."

Kissing her on the cheek, I swivel around her to see what she's cooking. "Ohh chicken and gnocchi?"

"You're favorite!" She sighs. "I wish you'd stop paying me. I'm married now, and you're my son! It's ridiculous."

"It would cost me twice as much to pay someone else, Ma. It's not a big deal." I shrug.

She shakes her head, moving back to my gigantic, stainless-steel stove and stirring the soup. "How was practice?"

I hop onto a barstool behind the large island and tell her about practice, it reminds me of when I was a kid. Except now I have my own 5,000 square foot house. "Oh, and then Coach asked me to donate myself for charity."

Her head snaps in my direction. "What?"

I laugh and tell her about the charity auction. She looks slightly relieved when I explain it, but still concerned. "I don't like it. Why do you have to go out with random women? Aren't you ever going to settle down?" A smile tugs at the corners of her lips. "Just look how happy me and Charlie are."

I grin at that. I love seeing her happy. She was crushed when my dad was unfaithful, I don't think she ever believed she'd fall in love again. But Charlie is probably the only man deserving of her. The guy is as close to a saint as you can get, working as a family advocate for the foster care system. They got married last year, and still act like they're on their honeymoon.

"I'm young, Ma. I have wild oats to sow," I say with a smirk. But I haven't been sowing any oats lately. The idea doesn't thrill me anymore.

She seems surprised at my answer. "You're about to turn thirty! I'd love to see you married to a nice girl and have some children. You'd be such a great father." Ma grows serious. "But you're not going to find your wife if you continue gallivanting around and being auctioned off like a Chip and Dale dancer!" She turns her back on me, annoyed again.

Yeah, I haven't *gallivanted* in a year. I can't even muster the desire to go out to bars and meet anyone. Maybe I really am getting old.

"Ma, chill out. It's an evening with an Eagle, not a date. Probably some old guy who's been an Eagles fan forever will win it. I'll skate around with them at the team's iceplex, we'll snap a few photos together, and it'll all be over. No big deal."

She purses her lips. "I hope you're right. Because there are a lot of crazy women out there with a lot of money to throw around."

"Always the protective mother." I smile fondly and she gives me a hesitant smile back.

"It's difficult to turn off the parenting-mode. Sorry."

"Maybe you and Charlie will have a few kids, then you'll be too exhausted to worry about me," I tease.

"I'm too old to have any more kids, Colby. Physically and mentally," she says with a forced laugh. We make eye contact for a brief moment before her gaze moves away from mine. I know we're thinking the same thing... Dad isn't too old to have children. Hence my baby sister.

It hurts my heart that Ma didn't meet Charlie sooner. She was the best mother anyone could ask for, and had her life gone differently, I think she would've had a whole brood of children.

I picture her as a grandmother as I watch her cook, seamlessly moving from bowl to bowl, mixing and stirring and sautéing. I can see her baking cookies with her grandkids, not caring about the mess.

An ache pangs in my chest, something that's becoming more and more familiar. An ache for a family of my own. A partner to share my life with, kids to fill the rooms in this big house. A family of my own.

A year ago, I was playing the game, thinking it was the time of my life. That I was in my prime. But I'm beginning to wonder if I was doing it all wrong. Spending a life with one woman isn't boring, it's poignant. It's like making it to the NHL, you work impossibly hard for it, and then strive to keep it. You focus every day on that one thing, put all your best effort in. I want that kind of relationship. I'm ready for it.

CHAPTER 4
NOEL

SATURDAY I quickly check the online portal to make sure my students have submitted their quizzes. We're a barely a month into the semester, and I don't have any research papers to read and grade yet. I'm soaking up my relaxing Saturdays while I still can.

Everyone has completed the quizzes I assigned, except for one of the athletes who tried to get me to extend the deadlines. I sigh. Why am I not surprised?

I know I shouldn't lump all athletes together in one big box... a box I'd label *irritating*. But it's also hard not to when they fail to prove themself different time and time again.

Weston Kershaw is the only one who keeps proving me wrong. And I'm happy about that... because if he broke my friend's heart, I'd never be able to beat him up for it. He's too big and muscular. Thankfully, he's a good guy, and he'd never hurt her.

Remy and Bruce seem alright too, though I don't know them that well. Mitch never smiles, but he does appear to make Andie happy. I won't hold his broody attitude against him.

But Colby Knight? Yeah, he'd be just like the hockey boys in my class, using his dimpled grin to get out of work.

Logging off my work computer in my office, which used to be Mel's room, I grab a book from one of my bookshelves and carry it into the living room to read. Right as I get comfy with a big, fluffy blanket, my phone rings with a FaceTime request. Glancing at my screen, I see it's my sister, Helen. My shoulders relax, she's the least dramatic of my siblings. Even though the two born in between us are boys. Yes, there are four of us.

You'd think there was nothing better to do in the tiny Maryland town I grew up in other than procreate... and you'd be right.

I answer the call, propping myself up on the couch. Helen's youthful grin comes into view, her face is softer and rounder than mine, but she looks a lot like me. Our brothers got their dark hair and dark eyes from my mom's side of the family. Me and Helen look similar to our dad's mom, Gram, when she was young. I can tell by the background that Helen is sitting on the front porch swing, the wind gently blowing her long blonde hair.

"Noel!" Helen squeals. She seems older since I saw her last month, maybe because she recently started her freshman year of high school.

"Are you wearing makeup?"

She glances away, rolling her lips between her teeth like I've embarrassed her. "Aren't you a bit young for makeup?" I add in a playful tone.

Helen rolls her eyes and huffs an annoyed breath, like I knew she would. "I'm not a baby! I'm in high school."

I can't help but laugh. Everyone thinks they're grown-up and mature when they're in high school, only to look back ten years later and cringe at how awful they were. Helen isn't awful, she's honestly the sweetest of us all. But she is immature, as you'd expect of someone at the young age of fifteen.

"I heard you're taking Gram to a fancy charity gala tonight." She looks away again, coiling a long, blonde ringlet around her finger.

"Ahh, that's what this is about." I pause, waiting for her to look back up. "I can't bring you to a work event with me, Helen. Not to mention you're almost two hours away, and Gram lives ten minutes from me."

"But it would be so fun to dress up!" She leans toward the phone, her eyes pleading.

The swing she's sitting on jostles and the youngest of our two brothers, Marcus, appears beside her. Landon is off at college in Delaware.

He leans in and waves at me, I can't help but smile at him. His dark hair is falling over his eyes Justin Bieber style, internally, I shake my head. "At least we get to go to homecoming!" Marcus says, obviously trying to cheer her up. "Homecoming wasn't even invented yet back in the olden days when Noel was in high school."

"Ha. Ha." I cross my arms. "Very funny."

"Going to a grown-up gala is *way* better than prom." Helen crosses her arms, mimicking me.

"All the hot girls in my class go to prom, so I'll agree to disagree." Marcus waggles his eyebrows, making us both laugh. For a moment, he reminds me of Colby... the dark hair, the devil-may-care attitude... I push the thought from my head.

Colby is full of two things: himself and testosterone. My adorable little brother isn't like that. I think...

"You're ridiculous," I tell him, but I'm still smiling.

"We're still on for the fantasy convention in a few weeks, right?" Helen asks, changing the subject.

Marcus snorts. "You two are giant nerds. You'll never have boyfriends."

I tense at his words, a small part of me wondering if they're true. Helen gives him a shove with her tiny arms, making me laugh. Marcus doesn't budge. Instead, he grins, trying to annoy her.

"We don't have boyfriends because we have standards, Marcus. Unlike you," Helen says.

"I don't have a boyfriend because I'm into girls," He retorts.

She sighs heavily. "You know I meant girlfriend. Please go away, this is a sister conversation."

He pushes up out of the swing, then leans in so I can still see him. "Fine. Talk to you later, sis." He winks and disappears.

"Anyway, the convention," Helen says, bouncing in excitement. "Did you get your Arwen cosplay?"

I nod, feeling pretty giddy myself. "Yes! Still waiting for my elf ears to arrive, but they should be here Monday."

"We're going to look so good."

I hear some rustling in the background and my parents appear on the screen. "Hi Noel!" Mom's dark hair is falling into her face since she's leaning over to look at the screen.

Dad swipes her hair out of her face. "Did I hear mention of a fantasy convention?"

Helen's eyes widen in panic. "It's just a sister thing, Dad."

He deflates. "Oh, right. Girl time." Dad chuckles.

"Nonsense!" Mom says. "Let's join them, I haven't seen Noel in over a month. And you've been wanting to see Gram, anyway." Mom pats Dad's cheek.

I get Helen's attention and shrug my shoulders. She doesn't appear thrilled about these additions to the fantasy convention.

That evening, I make the drive to Gram's glamorous townhouse in Alexandria. My parents have never understood why she didn't move closer to them after Grandpa passed, but I understand. This historical townhouse in the center of the hustle and bustle? It's her vibe, her life. She wouldn't be happy in a small town in Maryland, with no art exhibits, no new restaurants to try, no cherry blossoms in the spring.

Me and Gram get each other, we're kindred spirits. I'll never move back to Chester Bay either. It's a beautiful little town, and a great place to raise a family, but I'd slowly shrivel up and die of boredom.

Gram anticipated my arrival as usual, she's already on her front stoop, dressed as fabulously as I knew she'd be. I pull into the tiny parking spot allotted for her townhouse and step out of my 1957 Chevy Bel Air. At almost twenty-nine years old, most of the girls I grew up with have husband's and babies… I have Belle. My pride and joy. And with a dad who loves cars, she gets spoiled anytime she needs a tune up.

Stepping out of my car, I smile at Gram. "Hey, gorgeous. Did you have to go all out and make me look like chopped liver?"

She waves me off, but she's smiling. Her eyes crinkling adorably at the edges. "Oh, stop. I could never compete with a perky, young thing like you!"

Her rosy-pink chiffon gown drapes down to the ground, she doesn't want to show her feet since she can't comfortably wear heels anymore. A downside of having eighty-five-year-old feet.

The top of her gown is the same color but adorned with sparkly beads, the sleeves are slightly transparent and end at her elbows. Her white hair, which used to be as blonde as my own, is curled and backcombed to perfection. But that's nothing new. She did add a lovely gold clip above her right ear though. She's the epitome of class, as you'd expect from someone who spent half a lifetime as a senator's wife.

"You look absolutely beautiful, Noel," she tells me as I walk toward her to help her across the stone path. My deep red gown has a corset top with embroidered, white flowers. The skirt is simple, but it's a snug fit all the way down to my knees, making it difficult to take quick strides. The gold stilettos aren't helping either.

I finally reach Gram and hold on to her elbow. She shoos me away. "Stop treating me like an old woman!"

I laugh under my breath and remove my hand, instead walking ahead of her to open my passenger door. Gram slips inside, holding the bottom of her dress and pulling it into the car with her.

Once she's secure, I move to the opposite side, teetering on my heels. I'm pretty good with heels, but the worn, stone path is making things difficult.

Starting Belle up, we drive across town to the gala. It's at a five-star hotel in downtown D.C., and traffic is going to be atrocious.

When we're well on our way, Gram breaks the comfortable silence. "So, you wanna tell me why a beautiful, intelligent, sophisticated... single woman such as yourself asked her grandmother to be her date instead of a young, strapping man?"

I sigh. "I knew this was coming."

"You know, you can have a career you love during the day, *and* a man to keep you warm at night."

"Gram," I warn, but bite my bottom lip, trying not to laugh. "If you must know, there's a new professor at Arlington

University. I've been trying to get his attention for weeks, and nothing."

"An academic type?" she asks, her eyebrows furrowed slightly.

"Yeah, he even wears sweater vests." I sigh dreamily. "And he always has a book with him."

"Hmm."

"What?"

"Oh, nothing," she says, shaking her head and burrowing deeper into her seat.

"Just tell me. Your face hides nothing, Gram."

She laces her fingers together and places them gracefully on her lap. "It's just that... he sounds boring. And I think you need the opposite of boring, I think you need a pinch more spice."

I blow out a puff of air defensively. "Spice? My life has oodles and oodles of spice."

"No, it doesn't." She smiles at me. "You need someone adventurous. Someone who pushes you out of your comfort zone. Someone fun."

Stopping at a red light, I peer over at her, removing one hand from the steering wheel and laying it on top of her hands. "Like Grandpa?"

She looks off into space, she must be remembering their life together. "He was such a good man. I loved that we could laugh and have fun together."

The light turns green, and I give her hands a pat before accelerating again and focusing on the road. "Well, you can have fun but still have similar interests and personalities," I add.

Gram sways her head back and forth, obviously not convinced. "Just keep an open mind. Love might be where you least expect it."

———

I walk inside the ballroom, arm in arm with Gram and study the hotel ballroom. A room full of people I've never met before is an introvert's worst nightmare. Public speaking was my biggest concern about being a professor, but teaching students is different than speaking in front of my peers. It's not as intimidating.

I straighten my spine and keep walking, fighting the urge to run out of the room, go home, and curl up with a book.

Attending school in a small town was wonderful, everyone knew everyone, and for the most part, all the kids were nice. When I graduated early and went off to college, I didn't know mean girls existed… hadn't even seen the movie. My siblings, and my books, were my only friends.

College showed me there are a lot of people out there who won't mesh with you no matter what. Some personalities won't connect. And some people… are simply horrible.

I didn't enjoy the college experience at all… until I met Mel in the library during the first year of my doctoral program. Her kind smile instantly soothed something deep inside me. I could tell from that first meeting, we'd be friends. It helped that she was carrying one of my favorite books, Jane Eyre.

Gram's hand smooths over my own, I look over and find her studying me. "You've got this, sweetheart."

I give her a tight smile and we walk toward the center of the room, searching for our table. As we walk, I take a moment to appreciate the stunning ballroom. The D.C. Children's Hospital went all out with this event. Centerpieces full of colorful wildflowers adorn the center of each round table, the place settings are white and gold, matching nicely with the white tablecloths. The stage is lit with colorful lighting and two large floral arrangements that match the ones on the table.

There are even some children here, and a shorter table full of crayons and coloring pages to entertain them. Easels are arranged around the room with paintings of children on them, each one has a notecard telling a child's story.

"Oh, here we are." Gram's voice comes from my right side, I turn and see the place cards with our names on them. Pulling her seat out first, I make sure she's settled before taking my place beside her.

"If you would've brought a man, you could've been spoiled tonight instead of babying an old lady."

"Oh, stop it. You're my favorite person to hang out with and you know it."

She grins at that.

Our table fills up quickly, and soon, there's only one seat left. The emcee for the evening welcomes us and thanks everyone for attending, then the servers come around with the food. We had a choice of salmon, chicken, or vegan butternut squash soup. My chicken is cooked perfectly, and the sides of potatoes and asparagus are delicious too.

I glance at the one empty seat at the table once more, internally rolling my eyes that someone would be this late to a charity event.

A deep voice comes from behind me, and I jump. The familiarity of the baritone makes the tiny hairs on the back of my neck stand. The owner of the voice is obviously leaning in close to me, because I can feel his hot mouth close to my ear when he says, "Fancy meeting you here, angel."

CHAPTER 5
COLBY

RED IS HER COLOR. And not only because of her dress, but that angry blush on her face is sexy as hell. This woman being mad at me, is more enjoyable than any other woman being nice to me.

Maybe I should get in contact with the team therapist...

Noel stands abruptly, causing her chair to topple. I grab the chair with both hands and set it right. Noel whips around to glare at me. "What are *you* doing here?"

I'm momentarily speechless, now that she's standing, I can admire her red dress in its entirety. The structured top makes her look like a regency hottie, but the fabric on the bottom clings to her lithe body as if it was painted on. She's even taller than normal tonight, which means she's gotta be wearing some serious heels. Her lips are nearly in line with mine. It's almost too tempting.

"I was invited," I say with a shrug. That seems to annoy her even further.

A lovely, older woman seated beside her clears her throat loudly. "Noel, sweetheart. Who's your handsome friend?"

Her head whirls toward the woman. "Umm." She's at a loss for words. In Noel's mind, we're probably not friends... more like frenemies. "Gram, this is Colby Knight. You remember Mel's husband, West?" The woman nods, a pleasant smile on her face. "Colby is his teammate."

"Lovely to meet you, Mr. Knight. You can call me Gram."

I extend my hand and Gram shakes it. Turning her hand over, I bend and place a small kiss on the back. "Hello, Gram. You can call me Colby."

When I glance back up at Noel, I flinch. If looks could kill... I'd already be dead meat.

I peer behind her, noticing the empty seat on the side of the table and walk in that direction. Noel must not have read all the place cards, otherwise she would've expected me.

Noel slips back into her chair at the same time I do mine. She's trying so hard not to pay attention me, but let's face it... Me in a tuxedo? Hard not to stare.

I *almost* look as good as she does in that red dress.

Okay, not even close. But I *do* clean up pretty good.

"So, Colby, no date tonight?" Gram asks from across the table. The others at the table stare at me, then at Gram.

"Nope, I'm part of the auction. So, no date for me tonight."

"What do you mean, part of the auction?" Noel asks, finally meeting my gaze.

"You'll see." I wink. "Be sure to bid on me."

She scoffs, even though she doesn't know what I'm talking about. Noel has shields similar to mine, but where I act like a cocky, goofball... She pretends like she's in control and knows everything. Actually, I think it drives her crazy when she doesn't know something... and since she's highly intelligent, that probably doesn't happen often.

A server comes and places my meal in front of me, I'd

already informed them I'd be late. But my half-sister, Ruthie, had her third birthday party tonight, and I wanted to pop in via FaceTime before coming to the gala.

I dig into my food right away, starving since we had a long practice this morning. Coach nearly killed us. I check my watch; I need to be backstage in twenty minutes. Maybe I can fit one dance in with Noel... but she'll probably say no.

The rest of the guests at our table chat amicably, a few excusing themselves to dance. Noel's voice is the one I zero in on, I'm not paying attention to anyone else. Even though I keep my eyes averted, I can hear her soft conversation with her grandmother. She's sweet with her. Wish she was that way with me.

Quietly, I finally finish my food and check the time again. Thirteen minutes. Plenty of time for a dance. I stand and walk over to Noel and her grandmother. I know she senses my presence behind her, it's in the way her spine straightens, the way her shoulders set, and how she stops talking abruptly.

I stretch my hand out toward Gram. "Would you do me the honor of dancing with me?"

Gram's eyes twinkle for a second before she flinches and bends to rub her ankle. "Oof. I would... but my ankle has been giving me fits lately. Why don't you ask Noel instead?"

I grin and turn to Noel. "It's your lucky day, angel." I don't know why I provoke her this way... other than it's fun. "Would you do me the honor of a dance?"

Noel's lips set in a straight line; I can see in her eyes that her brain is working to come up with a reason to say no. But she waits too long to answer, and her Gram takes advantage of the opportunity.

"She'd love to! Go on. Don't deny this poor, dateless chap."

Noel's head whips back in her Gram's direction, I have an inkling she's glaring at her now, not so sweet anymore.

I really like this Gram lady. She's an awesome wingman. Er, wing woman… wing-grandma?

Gram and Noel have some sort of silent conversation where they just stare at each other, and only their facial muscles and eyebrows are ticking.

Noel must lose the silent battle, because she aggressively pushes out of her chair, almost making it topple over… again.

Women. Are. Fascinating.

The D.J. allows the current song to fade out, and a slow song swells through the speakers. I take Noel's hand in mine, noticing her fingers are nearly as long as my own. Just like her height, her hands are perfect for me. I practically drag her onto the dance floor. She hedges, peeking over her shoulder to Gram. Gram rolls her eyes and makes a gesture with her hand that seems to say, *don't you dare leave that man alone on the dance floor.*

While she's distracted, I wrap an arm around her waist, allowing it to rest in the arch of her back. She looks up at me and I'm struck by her height again. I barely have to tilt my chin to look right at her, and that makes me want to release a contented sigh. There's no straining my neck with Noel, I can gaze right into her caramel-colored eyes. She has to be around 5'10". That makes her only five inches shorter than me.

Tall guys always go for the petite girls. But they're really missing out. Honestly, the team P.T.s should warn the guys to find a partner similar in height, to save their necks… literally.

Speaking of necks, Noel is studying mine like it's the most interesting neck in the world. She's, once again, trying not to make eye contact. Her body is rigid in my arms.

"Why won't you look at me?"

Her eyes finally flit up to meet mine. "If I make eye contact, I might turn into a pillar of salt."

I nod. "Sodom and Gomorrah."

One side of her mouth twitches. "I'm surprised you know the reference."

"It's my favorite Bible story."

Her eyebrows shoot up. "What? Why?"

"It shows what happens when women don't take directions," I say flatly, knowing it will annoy the woman in my arms. And for reasons I can't quite understand, I enjoy seeing her ruffled.

She huffs and pulls away from me slightly. Her mouth opens to say some scathing remark, I'm sure. But I bring my hand up and place one finger over her luscious lips. They're soft under my touch, making me want to lean in and press my lips against them too.

"Shhhh. I know it's a good point. You don't have to flatter me."

She peeks her tongue out, poking my finger with the tip. It's a childish move, one that should deter me. But it makes her more fun, more unexpected. I remove my hand and slide it around to her lower back.

Noel heaves a sigh and grabs onto my arm, sliding said hand up a few inches on her back.

"So that's what you think? Women are pets, meant to sit down and shut up and allow men to tell them what to do."

"Of course not, I prefer them when they're licking my fingers."

She huffs indignantly, trying to pull away again. "I was *not* licking your fingers."

I tighten my arms around her waist, her hands going from my shoulders to my chest. I believe she's trying to put space between us, but her hands feel good on my chest. And my pecs happen to be one of my best features.

"Then what, pray tell, were you doing?"

She thinks for a moment, then her mouth quirks, like she's remembering something funny. "Me and my siblings used to do that. When one of them would put their hand over another's mouth and tell them to shut up, we'd just lick their hand, and they'd remove it instantly." Noel wrinkles her pert nose. "It's sort of gross now that I think of it."

I laugh. "How many siblings do you have?"

That question gets a genuine, beaming smile out of her. Note to self: she enjoys talking about her siblings.

"I have three."

"And let me guess... you're the oldest?"

She hesitates, biting her bottom lip. "What would make you think that?"

I breathe a small laugh through my nose, spinning her on the dance floor when the music swells. "You have oldest child written all over you. Driven, responsible, serious, and you have a perpetual stick up your butt."

"I do not have a," she lowers her voice to an angry whisper, "stick up my butt." Her jaw ticks, she's obviously offended.

"Don't worry, angel," I whisper back. "I happen to like your butt."

"You're a pig," she says, still annoyed, and trying to push away from me again. With an exasperated sigh, she changes the subject. "How many siblings do *you* have?"

"One," I answer, pulling her more tightly into my arms while she's distracted. She smells intoxicating... slightly spicier than usual. A cinnamon roll instead of a sugar cookie.

"And let me guess," She copies the words I said to her. "You're the baby."

My head drops back, and a booming laugh comes out of me, drawing the attention of the surrounding dancers. "Technically, I'm also the oldest."

"You're kidding."

I shake my head slowly from side to side. "I have a half-sister who's much younger than me. I was an only child most of my life."

"Oh." She seems surprised. "How much younger?"

"A *lot* younger."

"My youngest sister is only fifteen, the age gap can be weird, but also fun."

I smile, enjoying hearing her talk about her family. "Ruthie is three."

She gasps. "Three?"

I bite the insides of my cheeks to keep from grinning at her shocked expression. "My dad's girlfriend is much younger than he is."

"Goodness. She must be the same age as you."

"Younger."

Her pale, blonde eyebrows shoot up again. "Is that weird?"

I shrug, urging my mask to slip back into place. Complacent Colby with his careless attitude. Yeah, my dad started a new family. He left me and my mother to philander with women half his age. No big deal. "It used to be, but not anymore," I lie. "It's fun to have a little sister to spoil." That part isn't a lie, I do love spoiling Ruthie.

Her eyes are softer now, not in sympathy, but curiosity, perhaps?

I find myself wanting to talk more now that we're having a normal conversation. "I always thought it would've been fun to have a brother. Someone to play hockey with."

"Girls can play hockey too," she argues. "Maybe Ruthie will play hockey one day."

I grin at the thought of Ruthie with her bouncy, brown curls in a hockey helmet and little hockey skates and wonder if

Noel will ever meet her. The music stops and I reluctantly allow her to slide out of my arms.

I walk Noel back to the table, pulling her chair out for her. "Excuse me, ladies. But I'm needed for the auction now."

Noel studies me, her brow pinched in a confused expression, but Gram gives me a small wave and says, "Have fun!"

CHAPTER 6
NOEL

NOW THAT COLBY'S cologne isn't smacking me in the face, I can focus again. Cologne. Typical. I'm reminding myself cologne isn't my thing. I prefer men who smell like a bookstore... such as Dexter Hawthorne.

I sigh.

Or maybe who recently fought in a battle against Sauron. I'd even settle for a magical, high-fae type of scent. Nothing that can be bottled inside a department store and sold for an ostentatious amount of money.

Gram taps on my shoulder, pulling me from my stupor. "Sweetheart, the auction is starting. Do you have your number ready?"

Leaning over my chair, I find my formal clutch and pull it into my lap. I remove the paddle with an attached number card that we got when we signed in for the event and hold it up in the air so Gram can see. "Got it."

She places her own number on the table and gently puts her hand on my arm, forcing it down lower. "Careful, they're going to think you're bidding."

I laugh. "True."

A spotlight lands on the stage and peppy music plays as the emcee steps onto the stage. "Ladies and gentlemen, I'm Dr. Lehman, the president of the D.C. Children's Hospital. On behalf of the staff, families, and children that will benefit from your contributions this evening, I thank you for being here, and also for your generosity."

The room fills with applause, even the kids at the kids table are clapping and smiling.

"Now, let's get the fun started! Our first item up for auction is an all-expense paid vacation to the Napa Valley Luxury Spa and Winery. The bidding starts at one thousand dollars."

"Ohhh," Gram says, glancing at me with raised eyebrows before holding her paddle in the air.

"We have a thousand dollars from number eleven," Dr. Lehman says into the microphone before glancing at the other end of the room and stating, "And we have eleven hundred." His gaze shoots to another table again. "Twelve hundred!"

The bidding continues and Gram smirks. "That's alright, I have a feeling there will be something better to bid for as the evening goes along."

"They probably save the good stuff for last," I whisper. "I need to bid on something good for Arlington University."

Gram pats my hand that's not clutching the paddle. "We'll both leave with something good. I can sense it."

Gram and I wait as several vacation packages are auctioned off, as well as a speed boat and a few pieces of art. Finally, they bring out a painting by an up-and-coming American artist. It's a colorful depiction of a field full of bison with a giant blue sky above them. It will be perfect in the American history building. I bid on it and win with four-hundred dollars to spare.

I'm excited, and relieved, that I found the perfect item and stayed on budget, that I barely register when Dr. Lehman announces the next item up for auction. "Alright, get your paddles ready, you won't want to miss our next item!"

Colby walks onto the stage, that same confident swagger he always has, except it's tenfold tonight due to the tuxedo.

He is… stunning.

There's no other word for it.

Colby Knight was meant to wear a tuxedo; I reluctantly admit to myself.

"The D.C. Eagles were kind enough to donate an evening with an Eagle! That's right, our next winner will get to spend a night out with none other than Colby Knight himself."

Colby unbuttons his jacket, slides it off, and with one long finger drapes it over his back and does a pose for the crowd. Several whistles are blown around the room… mostly from women to be sure.

Dr. Lehman announces that the bidding will start at one-thousand dollars. I nearly have a heart attack when Gram is the first person to raise her paddle.

"Gram! What are you doing?" I try to grab her paddle away from her.

This is it; she's finally gotten so old that her mind has gone to mush. It's all downhill from here.

With the strength that's shocking for a woman her age, she yanks the paddle back out of my hand. "Leave me alone, you're going to make me lose." She huffs indignantly and bids again. The woman two tables away from us, who was the highest bidder, glares at Gram. Gram glares right back.

A new bidder, a man in his fifties, who's wearing a D.C. Eagles tie, outbids Gram.

The glaring woman bids again, then several more people. Colby is up to fifteen thousand dollars now, and Gram is sitting calmly in her seat.

The man with the Eagles tie is about to be announced as

the winner, Mr. Lehman is doing the whole, "Going once, going twice" routine.

Right when I think Gram has regained her sanity, and we're in the clear… she bids at the last second. Winning an evening with Colby for a whopping eighteen thousand dollars.

"Sold! To the lovely young lady at table nineteen!" Dr. Lehman sends Gram a wink, and Colby grins.

Colby exits the stage, and Gram turns toward me. She's beaming, her face is bright, appearing happier than I've seen her in a long time.

"Gram, what were you thinking?" I gape at her, seriously considering making her a doctor's appointment to get her brain checked.

"What's got your panties in a twist? This is the best eighteen thousand dollars I've spent in a long time." She relaxes in her seat, setting her paddle on the table.

"That's a lot of money, Gram."

She waves a hand. "I have plenty of money. You know what I don't have?"

"Uh… a boyfriend?"

She snorts a laugh through her nose. "Great grandchildren! *I* don't need a boyfriend, sweetheart. You do."

Realization hits me… she intends this evening with an Eagles player to be a set up… for me and Colby. Oh, absolutely not. "Gram."

"You're going."

"No. I'm not."

Her eyes go all soft and sad similar to a kitten. "It's my dying wish."

"You're not dying," I turn away from her, trying not to be affected by those sad grandma eyes.

"I am eventually," she says.

I look over at her again, her expression tells me she's totally serious, that she's not taking no for an answer.

Well, my gram is about to learn she's not the only stubborn woman in this family. Because I am *not* going out with Colby Knight.

———

Monday morning, I finish up my first lecture and check my phone once all of my students have filed out of the room. I have one missed call from Gram, another missed call from the Eagle's publicist to schedule my evening with an Eagle. I huff indignantly, causing a few curls to blow away from my face. I cannot believe Gram gave them my phone number...Okay, I can believe it. The woman has no boundaries, and she's apparently desperate for great grandchildren.

On top of the missed calls, I notice I also have five unread texts. Two from my group chat with Mel and Andie, and three from a number I don't recognize.

I open Mel's and Andie's first, thinking the others are either spam, or coupon codes from something I signed up for online.

MEL

Please, for the love of all that is holy, answer Colby's texts.

ANDIE

Yes, Noel, we are BEGGING YOU. *GIF of Puss n' boots' pouting face*

"Colby's texts? He doesn't even have my number..." I mumble to myself. My eyes widen when I realize that he must've gotten my number from the publicist. I know Mel and

Andie wouldn't give him my number. Solidarity and all that. Hoes before bros.

Exiting out of the group chat, I pull up the text thread from the unknown number.

UNKNOWN
Hey, angel.

I groan out loud.

UNKNOWN
You know any other woman would be dying to go out to dinner with me, right?

UNKNOWN
It's just dinner. I know you love to eat. And it's free.

NOEL
Actually, it cost $18,000.

COLBY
The 18 grand was a charitable donation, you know, for the CHILDREN.

COLBY
An evening with yours truly is an added bonus. I'll even stay the night with you, free of charge, because I'm feeling generous. *GIF of Jimmy Fallon winking*

NOEL
I'm not going on a date with you.

COLBY
It's not a date... it's an evening with an Eagle.

NOEL

Well, Gram won the auction, therefore she's
the one having "an evening with an Eagle."

The phone in my hand rings unexpectedly and I almost
drop it. Colby is calling me. I hate it when people do this. I tap
the phone screen to answer, but only so we can finish this
conversation and he'll quit texting me... and Mel... and
Andie.

"What, Colby?"

"Good morning, Dr. Woodcock." He enunciates the last
half of my name that way he always does.

I exhale a deep breath through my nose and rest my back-
side against my desk, crossing my legs at the ankles. "You
really like my last name, don't you?"

"Not as much as I like mine." He pauses, and when he
speaks again, I can hear the smile in his deep voice. "I could
give you my last name, you know."

"Colby," I warn, losing my patience.

I hear him sigh through the phone. "You Woodcock women
are impossible. Gram refuses to schedule our evening out,
telling the publicist to contact you... but guess what? You
won't schedule a time either. You two sure know how to disin-
tegrate my man card."

Glancing up at the high ceiling in the lecture hall, I shake
my head. "I think your man card was swiped one too many
times and disintegrated itself."

His deep laugh filters through the speaker. "You know, I
don't do this often, but I'm willing to offer you unlimited
swipes to my man card."

I groan loudly.

"Okay, okay. I'll stop." I can hear him take a deep breath.
"You know we're supposed to take pictures of our evening for

the Children's hospital, right? What am I supposed to do, photoshop someone in the photo?"

A twinge of guilt hits me. But more than guilt, I'm annoyed with Gram. She should've let one of those other people win, someone who really wanted to go to dinner with Colby. This isn't Colby's, or my, fault.

"My birthday is Friday... you wouldn't make me go to dinner alone on my birthday, would you?"

I purse my lips, knowing I'm stuck going to dinner with him or I'll come across as a huge jerk. "Fine."

"Yes!" He exclaims, causing me to hold the phone away from my now ringing ear.

"Text me the details. And don't call me again."

"I'm glad you're as excited about our date as I am," he teases.

"It's not a date," I say, then hang up before he can argue.

"What's not a date?"

I jump in surprise at the sound of a decadent British accent. Lifting up off my desk, I glance at the doorway and see Dexter Hawthorne resting against the doorframe. His vest today is a brown tweed with wooden buttons, paired with matching trousers. This man could make anything look good... actually, Dr. Hawthorne in Legolas cosplay? Say less.

"Oh, ha. It's nothing." I look down at my feet and tuck a curl behind my ear. Wait, why am I doing staring at my feet? I'm a confident, well-educated woman, I will meet his gaze and square my shoulders, I don't care how closely related this man might be to Prince William.

He shoves off the doorframe and takes a step inside the lecture hall. "I stopped by to speak with you about a few students trying to transfer from your class to mine."

I sniff haughtily. "Let me guess, the hockey scholarship guys?"

"How did you know?" His eyebrows pinch together.

I grab my purse and pull it over my shoulder. "They talked to me about extending deadlines for the research paper."

"Ah." His perfect mouth pulls into a smirk. "And you wouldn't work with them?"

I stand taller, not wanting to back down. But I don't want him to think I'm mean either. In my most relaxed voice, I ask, "You think I should extend my deadlines for athletes?" I pause. "But what about the other students? It doesn't seem fair."

He bows his head slightly, agreeing with my point. "No, I agree. It's simply that the D1 scholarship students follow an extremely rigid training program, you could go a *smidge* easier on them," he says.

"Just because they can hit a small circle into a big net, doesn't mean they get more time to complete their assignments." I cross my arms, trying to appear confident instead of annoyed.

He chuckles light-heartedly and I relax.

I meet his gaze and remind myself to tone it down a bit. *Be nice, Noel. You're too brash, which is probably why he's never asked you out.*

I clear my throat and smile at him... I'm hoping that'll make him think I was joking. "I'm sure they'll be happy to have their degree to fall back on if they ever get injured."

"Dr. Woodcock, do you play sports?" he asks, his face still calm.

I shrug a shoulder lazily, pretending I was expecting the question. "Of course," I answer quickly. "I lift weights."

By lifting weights, I mean I sleep with a weighted blanket. The look of surprise on his face is priceless, so I'm not admitting that last part to him. I mean, I *have* lifted weights. Andie made me and Mel try it out during one of our girls' nights. It was horrible.

His eyes quickly dip down my body then back up. When his gaze meets mine again, I'm expecting a heated look, like the one Colby gives me when he blatantly checks me out. Instead, Dexter only looks unconvinced that I lift weights. Apparently, my tall, gangly form doesn't do it for him. For a moment I feel self-conscious... or maybe just annoyed that I'm attracted to Dr. Hawthorne, but he looks at me like he would look at his mother, or little sister.

Taking a moment to study him the way he did me, I realize he's just as tall and gangly. Pot, meet kettle. "Do *you* play sports?"

Internally, I berate myself again. Chill, Noel. This is not how to get a nice, intelligent man to ask you out. Be calm, be poised. WWKMD? (What would Kate Middleton do?) That's probably the type of woman he prefers.

He grins. "Of course, I was on scholarship at university."

"For what?" My voice comes out louder and more unbelieving than I wanted it to. That certainly wasn't a Kate Middleton response. Dexter will never see me as a dateable woman at this rate. My words have always come out too freely... guys don't like that. Except Colby, he seems to thrive on my word vomit. What a creep.

"Pickleball."

I snort a laugh before I can hold it in. When I take in his offended expression, I disguise my laugh as a cough. "Right. That's cool." I raise my eyebrows, trying to appear impressed. "Did you find it difficult balancing your pickleball schedule and your homework?"

He shifts on his feet. "No, I didn't. And as you said, I'm grateful I kept up with my studies since I wasn't a career-athlete."

Can you have a career as a pickleball athlete?

I change the subject, "Right, I know you're a fantastic history teacher, and they're welcome to transfer to your class."

Good job, Noel. I'm giving myself an imaginary pat on the back. Guys love compliments. Dexter's shoulders straighten and his chin lifts slightly, I believe he's preening. Since the compliment went well, I continue, "I'm a fair teacher, and I've given them plenty of time to complete everything. If they don't procrastinate, it shouldn't be an issue."

Dexter... er, Dr. Hawthorne's chin tips down again, in a subtle nod. "Alright then. Well, enjoy your date."

I blink a few times in surprise before remembering he overheard the end of my call with Colby. I open my mouth to respond but before I can, he turns on his heel and walks out of my classroom. His tall form quickly disappearing around the corner.

I sigh, closing the door behind me. Should I be more lenient about deadlines? Colby's comment about having a stick up my butt pops into my head. I remind myself I'm a professor, not a babysitter. But there's still a lingering tightness in my chest, the inkling that I need to change something or do something to make myself more likable. Then perhaps, I'd be more attractive to the opposite sex.

What do all the girls in my books have that I don't have? Why am I the uptight spinster instead of the cool girl who catches the attention of the most eligible bachelor from across the ballroom?

Is being a chill, cool girl what attracts guys like Dexter? How can I be so confident and accepted by my friends, but so absolutely misunderstood by men?

My eyes prick with tears. I swallow them back. Crying over this is absurd. I need to find a book on the topic and study. Studying has never let me down.

A thought pops into my head... I know the perfect person to help me with this. Someone who knows everything there is to know about attraction and dating and what draws a man in.

Who needs study material when you have a real-life dating expert.

Colby Knight, you're finally about to do something besides drive me crazy.

CHAPTER 7
COLBY

"HAPPY THIRTIETH BIRTHDAY, GRANDPA," Bruce says as he steps out of his beat-up old Chevy. We're in the parking lot of the children's hospital to visit the kids. We visit once a month as part of the Eagles' community outreach program, and we bring toys for the kids. I usually drop by and visit an extra time or two though, because I love seeing how the kids are doing.

I'm carrying a large duffle bag full of D.C. Eagles stuffed animals, but I pretend I'm holding a cane instead, and start walking the way an old man would. "Boy howdy, young man. I think I forgot my dentures."

He studies my mouth. "Naw, your teeth still look great. Thank goodness for implants."

I snort a laugh and throw an arm around his shoulders. "No joke. We'd all be toothless."

"Speak for yourself, mine are all real." He waggles his blond eyebrows.

"Maybe we all should wear goalie masks."

He ponders for a second, then nods. "Wouldn't hurt."

We enter the large sliding doors at the front of the hospital then walk to the front desk. Norris, an older gentleman who mans the desk, recognizes us and smiles. "Good to see you both, how's training going?"

Bruce grins. "We're working hard, man. But I love it. Happy to be back on the ice."

He hands us our badges and we slide the lanyards around our necks before taking the elevator up to the cancer treatment floor. When Tom Parker, the Eagles' general manager, first asked me to volunteer with the children's hospital, I was hesitant. I knew it would be sad, seeing the sick kids. But that first day I realized how much joy we brought them by visiting, and it brought me joy too.

It would suck to be stuck in the same room for weeks, or even months at a time. Our visits break up their time here and give them something to look forward to. Half of them don't even know who we are, they're simply thrilled to have a new face to look at.

When we step off the elevator, Nurse Becky greets us. She thinks she's my number one fan... but she's one of a million. This is probably why I'm drawn to a certain professor. The one and only woman who doesn't think I have rainbows shooting out of my ass.

"Hi, Colby." She looks up at me with her sweet smile. She has a freckled nose and two reddish, blonde braids that hit right at her shoulders. "And Bruce!" she adds on.

Bruce shoots me a side eye before she can see it. Bruce tells me I'm an attention whore, and he doesn't get any chicks when I'm around. I tell him chicks aren't into blonds. Then we fight and go round and round about it. It's our thing.

We turn our attention back to nurse Becky and smile at her before she ushers us toward the first room. We usually trail her as she makes her rounds. The kids who haven't seen us before always seem comforted by her presence.

We come to the first room; I know this one. It's Broderick, a six-year-old boy with leukemia. His face lights up when we walk inside. I shake the duffle bag I've been carrying, and he claps his hands together.

"Hey, bud. You get first pick of the goodies today," I tell him, unzipping the bag and coming toward him. His parents are on the little sofa in the corner of the room, smiling as they watch.

He takes a quick peek at the various stuffed animals, choosing a stuffed eagle clothed in a number twenty-seven jersey... my number.

"Great choice, man!" I wink at him, knowing Bruce is right beside me, probably annoyed.

"You know, Broderick..." Bruce grabs an eagle from the bag, one that's wearing his own number thirty-nine, and sits at the foot of the hospital bed. "Goalie is arguably the most important position on a hockey team."

Broderick glances between the two eagles; I note his new cap is made from D.C. Eagles fabric and smile to myself.

"It's a really hard choice."

Bruce chuckles and hands him the Eagle in his hand. "You can have both. Our little secret, okay?"

The boy's dark eyes widen. "Really? Okay, I won't tell."

Bruce pretends he's locking up his mouth and throwing away the key, pulling a hearty laugh from Broderick. It's the best sound. I glance at his parents; his mom's eyes are filled with tears and his dad has his arm around her. I wonder if Broderick's laughter isn't something they get to hear often.

We talk to Broderick about preseason training camp and who our first game is against before he starts yawning. Nurse Becky gets our attention, nodding once so we know it's time to let him rest and head to the next room.

The next room is a little girl, probably around the age of

ten. I haven't seen her before, but she's wearing a wig that's bright pink and makes her blue eyes pop. There's a woman seated in an armchair beside her bed, she has the same blue eyes so I'm assuming it's her mom.

I peek at the dry erase board to find out her name as I walk to her bedside. "Well, hello there Emma."

She smiles bashfully then looks down at her blanket. "Hi," she whispers, peering up at us for a second.

Bruce rests his hip against the bed and grins at her. "Your hair is awesome. Do you think mine would look cute in that color?"

She purses her lips together, trying not to laugh. But shakes her head slowly from side to side.

Bruce gasps and puts a hand to his chest. "I'm hurt, Emma."

Emma and her mom giggle. Bruce grabs the duffle from me and takes out an eagle with his number on it, thrusting it into her lap before she can choose a different one. "Number thirty-nine. That's me."

"Thank you," she says, picking up the bird and snuggling it to her chest.

Bruce looks back at me and grins. I shake my head but can't help the smile that tugs at my lips.

We take a few minutes to talk to Emma and her mom before nurse Becky grabs our attention and takes us to the next room.

We do this for two hours. It's fun and sad... and emotionally exhausting. I feel selfish even thinking that, because I can't imagine how hard cancer treatment is on these kids and their families. Being a bright spot in their day is an honor.

When Bruce and I walk into the parking lot toward our vehicles, our duffle bag now empty, he turns to me. "What are your plans for your birthday?"

"Finally have a date with Noel."

He stops in his tracks and gasps. "No way!"

I shimmy my head back and forth. "Well, kind of... sort of."

"Explain." We come to a stop in front of Bruce's pickup, and he slumps against the driver's side door.

I tell him about the auction that Coach Young wrangled me into and how Gram bid on me. By the end he's laughing so hard his face is bright red.

"And now she has to go out with you?" He breaks into another fit of laughter. "That's brilliant. You owe Gram a favor."

I laugh along with him. "Don't I know it."

"Where are you taking her? Are you heading straight to the courthouse and sealing the deal?"

Bringing my thumb and forefinger to my chin, I thoughtfully say, "Great idea. I could kidnap her."

He snickers. "Actually, isn't that a plot from an audiobook Mitch accidentally listened to?"

"Accidentally," I say with air quotes. We both laugh at Mitch's expense. "Anyway, since it's my birthday I'm taking her to dinner, and then to do one of my favorite activities."

He snorts. "We all know what your favorite activity is, and there's no way Noel is going to be down for that. She'll slap you for even mentioning it."

"*That's* not my favorite activity! Do you even know me at all?"

He arches an eyebrow, appearing unconvinced.

"When's the last time you saw me with a woman?"

He opens his mouth to answer then closes it. Opens it again, then closes it. He bites his bottom lip as he thinks. "You know what, it's been a while since I saw you with anyone."

"Exactly. So, stop slut-shaming me."

He punches my shoulder. Hard. "Well, look who's growing up! Proud of you man."

I roll my eyes. "We're all young and wild at some point."

He laughs. "What's this favorite activity you speak of?"

"Bungee jumping," I say, throwing my hands up in frustration. He's even gone with me before.

"Oh! Right. Yeah, sorry." He smirks. "You think she'll be down for that?"

"I think she likes to look tough, and with the publicity team there... she won't be able to chicken out."

He blows out a breath. "You're a brave man. Good luck."

I glance down at my wristwatch. "I'll see you at training camp in the morning. Gotta go get ready for my date."

———

Noel walks toward me, a sassy expression clouding her face. The all-too familiar way she always looks at me. I told her to dress casually, and she's gorgeous in some distressed jeans, white sneakers, and a fitted white top. "Really? Pancake Palace?"

"It's *my* birthday," I say, taking her arm and gently sliding it through mine before leading her through the sticky, mostly yellow restaurant. When we arrive at my favorite corner booth, I let go of her and give a gentlemanly bow. "Ladies first."

"Eighteen thousand dollars, and all I get is Pancake Palace," she mutters, sliding into the booth, as far away from me as possible. "Is this area of town even safe?"

I slide in right next to her. "I offered to pick you up."

She makes a show of glaring down where my body is almost pressed against hers, then eyes the large portion of the empty booth behind me. I acquiesce and scoot about a foot away from her, giving her some space. My jeans rub against the pleather, making a gross noise.

A waitress comes over to our table, we're the only ones here, and hands us two greasy, laminated, yellow menus. I haven't seen this waitress before, she's probably forty and dressed in the Pancake Palace uniform, a 1950s style dress, with a small white apron.

"What can I get y'all to drink?" she asks, realization dawning on her when she finally looks at me. "Oh, my good-ness! You're Colby Knight!" she yells, then squeals.

Thank goodness no one else is here tonight. I'd be swarmed. Todd, the owner of the restaurant, normally instructs his staff to play it cool. One of the reasons I love coming here. That, and the twenty-four-hour, all you can eat breakfast buffet.

Sure enough, Todd runs out of the kitchen, looking like an angry father about to go into a lengthy lecture. "Sara! We talked about this." His hands are on his hips.

She stares down at her yellow shoes that match her dress perfectly. "I'm so sorry. I know you warned us he comes in sometimes but seeing him in person still took me by surprise!" She gawks at me, open-mouthed, one more time. "He's so beautiful," she whispers. "He's too pretty to be real."

Todd points toward the kitchen, and she snaps out of her trance, then sloughs off like a pouting teenager.

"Very sorry about that Mr. Knight. What can I get you and this lovely lady to drink?"

"Coffee for me, my usual cinnamon roll creamer," I tell him then glance at Noel.

She's studying me with a bemused, and perhaps fasci-nated, expression. "I'll have coffee as well, please," she says while still studying me.

"I'll get those right out. Two buffets?"

"I'd like the buffet, yes. How about you Noel?"

She nods. "I'll have the buffet too." She hands him our menus and he smiles at her before heading back toward the kitchen.

I clap my hands together and slide out of the booth. "They have plates at the buffet, let's go get some grub."

She slips out on the opposite side of the half-circle and follows me toward the buffet area in the next room. The small island is lit from above with yellow lights that match the rest of the decor, and heated trays line the table. The trays are steaming and filled with everything from pancakes and waffles to bacon and sausage.

Noel huffs out a small laugh, still staring at me like I grew two heads.

"What?" I ask incredulously.

"This is all so…" She pauses like she can't think of the right word. "Surprising."

I arch an eyebrow, a silent plea for her to continue.

"Okay, I've been around West and Mitch enough to know they're quite particular about their diets. But then you're over here—" She trails off, gesturing with one hand at the plate I've already filled with waffles.

"I train hard, I'm always starving!"

She laughs again. "You're not worried about your performance and muscle mass?"

"Oh, angel." I lean in close. "My performance, and my mass, are just fine."

She swipes two waffles off my plate and places them on hers. My jaw drops. In all my days, I've never… ever… had a woman steal my food. No one has dared. I'm not sure I'm a fan of it.

"Oh, stop looking at me like I've ruined your birthday. I have to get my eighteen thousand worth."

"You're a monster," I deadpan, but she walks away from me, filling her plate like she's done nothing wrong.

"You know how Joey from Friends doesn't share food?"

"Yeah, yeah." She rolls her eyes. "Let me guess... Colby doesn't share food either?"

"That smart doctor brain of yours sure figures things out fast."

She looks up like she's about to say something but her attention snags on something behind me. "You've got to be kidding me." She sets her place down and walks over to where a large photo of me hangs on the yellow wall.

She reads the plaque below the framed photo, out loud, "From Knight to Pancake Palace Prince! Colby Knight breaks the record for most pancakes eaten in one hour."

The picture was taken a year ago, I have a napkin tucked into the neck of my t-shirt and I'm grinning. There's even a sprinkle of powdered sugar on my chin.

Noel peeks over her shoulder at me. "Sometimes I can't wrap my mind around the fact that you're a successful adult."

CHAPTER 8
NOEL

COLBY and I are seated back at the booth now. The waitress that gawked at him earlier keeps peeking her head out of the kitchen and staring. Colby's angled away from her and doesn't appear to notice.

I watch as he dumps six little cinnamon roll creamer tubs into his coffee until it's practically white.

"What?" he asks, looking up and noticing how I'm watching him. "You don't use creamer?"

"I do use creamer. But I prefer to taste the coffee also."

"The taste of coffee is overrated. It's just a warm substance to pour yummy creamer into."

I shake my head; this man always leaves me stumped for words. Glancing down at my enormous plate of food, my mouth nearly salivates. I add some butter and syrup to my stack of waffles and dig in, shoving a large bite into my mouth. The perks of being on a not-date, you can be messy.

"I love how much you eat," Colby says before guzzling half of his creamer-coffee. "I hate seeing girls pick at their food, like that's going to make them more appealing somehow."

I swallow down my bite. "It's ladylike to eat like a bird." I pick up my coffee cup gently, making sure my pinkie is out, then take a dainty sip.

Colby throws his head back with a hearty laugh.

"Speaking of girls..." I hedge, poking my fork into the pile of food on my plate.

Colby calms down and wipes at his mouth with his napkin. "Okay..."

I shift in my seat, suddenly feeling awkward and uncomfortable. It's then I realize, I've actually felt at ease here with Colby. I think I was even enjoying myself. Like we were something akin to... friends.

"I could use your expertise in the relationship department," I blurt before I can chicken out.

Colby stares blankly back at me for what seems like a whole minute. He finally breaks the silence. "You think I'm a relationship expert?"

"Not a relationship expert, but perhaps, an expert on what makes men and women attracted to one another. And maybe even"—I swallow, my throat feeling thick—"how to *do* the attracting."

His eyebrows shoot up to the thick, dark waves resting on his forehead. "You don't think you're attractive?"

I roll my eyes. "It's not that I think I'm unattractive. It's just. Well—"

"Spit it out, Noel." He sets his now-empty coffee mug on the table.

I blow out a breath. "There's this guy I have a crush on. At work. But he looks at me like I could be his sister. I think I'm too brash. I don't know how to get him to notice me. I was hoping maybe you could help me."

Something passes over Colby's usual jovial expression so quickly, a split second of what appeared to be malevolent anger. But he'd have no reason to be angry about this. I'm probably wrong. I know Colby has always flirted with me, but he's a flirt. That's what he does. It's nothing serious, nothing he'd get jealous over.

He slowly picks up his fork and knife and cuts into his stack of waffles and pancakes. Not sure why he needed both, but it's a tall stack. He looks thoughtful as he works. I stay silent, waiting for his response.

Colby finally looks at me, his mouth set in a line. Completely serious. "Why would you want to get the attention of a guy who's stupid enough not to notice you to begin with?"

I'm taken aback by his comment, and for a second, I wonder... Why do I? But then I remember Dexter Hawthorne; the set of his lean shoulders, his vests, the accent, how he exudes intelligence and grace.

I bristle, feeling defensive of Dexter. "He's not stupid. I'm just not great around guys I'm attracted to. I get all weird and awkward and opinionated."

Colby snuffs a laugh. "Angel, you're always free with your thoughts and opinions. Why does that have to be a bad thing?"

"It's not a *bad* thing," I say. "Some people may need more time to adjust to it, though."

He rests an elbow on the table, holding his fork loosely in his hand. "Do you realize how absolutely infuriating it is to be around women who feed me whatever they think I want to hear? Who flatter me constantly?"

"Oh yeah," I tell him sarcastically. "That sounds horrible. All guys hate that, I'm sure."

"They should. It's stupid. I could be the world's biggest asshole and women would still hang all over me. It gets old."

I heave a heavy sigh. "Can you quit humble bragging? This conversation is about me."

He laughs. "I'm not bragging. It's genuinely annoying." He leans back in his seat, draping one long, tanned arm across the back of our booth. "My point is, if that's what this guy wants… for women to stroke his ego, maybe he's not the guy for you."

Crossing my arms, I slump back in the booth. "You've got Dexter all wrong. And I'd like the chance to get to know him better."

"Dexter?" Colby's eyebrows shoot up.

"Yes. Dr. Dexter Hawthorne," I say on a dreamy sigh. "He's British."

Colby wrinkles his nose, unimpressed. "He sounds too wimpy for you."

"Academics are *not* wimpy."

He shrugs one of his firm looking shoulders. A sweater-vest would never fit Colby. "Whatever you say. Does he watch hockey?"

"Hockey appreciation is the last thing on my list of things I'd look for in a future partner." I lean forward, grabbing a few blueberries off my plate, and popping them into my mouth. "And if you must know, he's quite an athlete."

"Oh, really?" he asks in that infuriatingly cocky voice of his.

"Yes." I turn my nose up. "He was on scholarship at university," I repeat what Dexter told me, and try not to grimace afterward.

"For what? Water polo?" He snickers.

"Pickleball," I mutter quietly before stuffing another bite of waffle into my mouth.

Colby nearly rolls out of the booth. I've never seen a person laugh this hard.

Annoyed, I ignore him while I finish my plate of food. I've nearly finished my meal by the time he gets his laughter out.

He quietly finishes his plate, but chuckles to himself the entire time. I've never met a more infuriating, childish person.

Do his looks alone really get him all the girls? How can they stand his personality?

Before I brought Dexter up, I thought we were having a decent time. Probably the first time I've ever enjoyed Colby's company. But now he's ruined it with his incessant laughter and poking fun at my future husband. Okay, maybe not my future husband. But future date, hopefully.

"Noel," Colby says, reaching his hand across the table and tapping the back of my hand. My eyes dart to Colby's. I realize I've been totally zoned out, deep in thought, for who knows how long. "I'm sorry for laughing. It's just… pickleball." He chuckles again. "And also, the idea of *you* needing help to get this guy's attention is absurd."

"Well, I do." I shrug my shoulders. "And it was humiliating to even ask."

"Listen." He sighs. "I'll try to help, okay? But I'm not a relationship expert…and I don't think this guy is worth your time."

"You're an expert in getting, and keeping, the attention of the opposite sex. And that's what I need."

Colby picks up his paper napkin and wipes his mouth. "We'll talk about the details at our next destination."

"Next destination? I did not agree to this."

He arches a brow. "Do you want my help or not?"

I glare at him. "Fine."

CHAPTER 9
COLBY

NOEL INSISTED on driving herself to our next location, and I was surprisingly relieved. I need a minute to process the fact that she not only likes someone who isn't me, but is so desperate for his attention that she's willing to ask me for help with it.

The last thing I want to do is help her get some other guy's attention... but if I play my cards right, this could work to my advantage. She will have to talk to me, and even spend time with me, if I'm helping her. She'd owe me.

Dr. Noel Woodcock owing me a favor is quite possibly the most power I will ever hold.

I pull to a stop at a red light and close my eyes, willing myself to relax. Hoping to calm down before I arrive at the Action City Ziplining and Bungee Jumping, and I only have like two more blocks to compose myself. "Only an idiot wouldn't notice Noel," I tell myself in the rearview mirror. "This guy is the biggest moron to ever walk the planet."

The light turns green, and I continue driving until I pull into the parking lot near the bungee and zipline course. Noel must have a lead foot, because her drool-worthy classic car is already parked in the lot. I bring my Mercedes Benz G-Wagon to a stop beside it. Noel steps out of her car, and I don't miss the way her eyes peruse my G-Wagon. If only she'd look at *me* that way.

Opening my door, I hop out of the SUV and close the driver's door, then lean against it. Draping one arm across my baby, I smolder at Noel. "You know, me and G are a package deal."

She groans. "You're impossible. Aren't you supposed to be helping me make Dr. Hawthorne fall in love with me?"

The reminder makes my stomach coil. "Right." I huff a laugh. It sounds forced. I remind myself that helping her with this will allow us to spend time together. Then maybe she'll realize I'm her Knight in shining armor. I snicker at my own pun.

"What's so funny?" Noel asks, crossing her arms.

I clear my throat. "Nothing."

My hand finds its way to the small of her back, and I lead her in the direction of the trail that will lead us to the bungee platform. It's a bit of a walk since it's out in the forest where the trees are taller.

"Alright, angel. We've got about thirty minutes before the team's publicist starts photographing your evening with an Eagle."

She scoffs. "You didn't want them photographing us at the Pancake Palace?"

I stare at her, growing serious. "Of course not. The Pancake Palace is special." She studies me like she can't tell if I'm joking. I'm not. I've never taken anyone to that place before, not even my teammates. It's the place I can go and have everyone leave me be, a secret spot no one else knows about. It's just for me. And now, Noel. But I'm not telling her that. I can't play all my cards just yet. Especially when she *thinks* she wants some other guy. Slapping my usual cocky smile back on my face, the one that hides what I'm truly feeling, I say, "Plus, people will eat this up."

She ignores the cocky facade the way she always does. "What's so great about ziplining? That's what we're doing, right?"

I shrug. "Sure."

She ignores my vague response. "Do you like being photographed? I'm sure you're quite the model."

I take a long stride to get in front of her then spin to face her, making her stop in her tracks and look up at me. "You think I'm handsome enough to be a model?"

She rolls her eyes and tries to push past me, but I keep her where she's at by gently grabbing her arms. "It's the dimples, isn't it?" I ask, trying to ignore how soft her warm skin beneath my hands.

The physical contact makes me not only feel warm all over but makes me want things I shouldn't want. Does she seriously not feel this?

Tugging out of my grasp, she scurries past me, continuing on the trail.

With a few long strides, I catch up to Noel. We walk in comfortable silence beside each other, and she matches me stride for stride, easily keeping up with me. Our classic cars, our long strides, our love of food... we're the perfect match.

She's the spicy cinnamon to my roll. The book to my worm. The angel to my... demon?

"Don't you have to pose for a lot of promotional stuff?" Noel asks, glancing up at me briefly.

"Yeah, we do. It's fun, actually. But on media days, I get to enjoy interacting with everyone I don't usually see. Like our social media team. It's a good time to get to know everyone."

"What's your least favorite part of your job?" she asks, taking me by surprise. No one ever asks me that.

I think for a minute before answering. "Being recognized everywhere I go. Sometimes I wish I could go into Target and grab some shampoo without anyone asking for a photo. When I'm at an event, or at a game, I don't mind that... because I'm in work mode." I sigh. "But when I want to be normal, I can't."

She nods in understanding. I don't know how she pulls these honest answers out of me, but I always show more of my true self around her than I do other people.

"As an introvert, I would hate that, too. Being around a lot of people I don't know wears me out. That's how my book obsession began. As a kid, that's how I would unwind after school." She smiles down at the dirt path.

I love seeing her smile. It's a nice change from the glare she usually sports when I'm around. "What was your favorite book as a kid?"

"Lord of the Rings," she answers quickly. "It was my first fantasy, and I was hooked. I re-read it every year; you never forget your first love." She sighs contentedly, and I think to myself that I could listen to her talk about books all damn day.

I could listen to her talk about anything. I imagine her presenting a lecture to her students, how captivated she must keep an audience. She's passionate about the things she loves, and the people she loves. Noel has more depth than anyone I've ever known. There are endless layers to get through.

"Do you like to read?" she asks, and I realize I've been quietly thinking for several minutes.

I quirk my mouth to the side. "I haven't read a book in ages. I'd like to, though. What would you recommend?"

She goes into serious professor mode, and it's hot as hell. "*The Hobbit* is a great place to begin if you want to try fantasy. Tolkien is literally the grandfather of all fantasy works. Jane

Eyre is excellent historical fiction. Really, you just need to think about what excites you and give it a try." She glances up at me, her caramel-colored eyes shining brightly. "And if you don't have time to sit and read a physical book, audiobooks are a great option too. I know Mitch loves audio."

I chuckle at that. "That's a good idea, I should try that. I have a hard time sitting still too long."

We come to a stop as we reach the platform, and it hits me that we just had a whole conversation without fighting. Or me making an inappropriate flirtatious comment. Something like hope swirls in my gut. Maybe I could win her over, after all.

CHAPTER 10
NOEL

"NO. ABSOLUTELY NOT," I tell Colby as we stare up at a platform built for bungee jumping.

And here I was, only a moment ago thinking, *wow, I'm enjoying my time with Colby Knight. He's being so normal and lovely.* But it was all a trick.

"Oh, come on. The camera crew is all ready to go, and the fans will love it."

"*Your* fans!" I throw my hands up.

Colby holds out a waiver, one that I'm supposed to sign. There are two young men waiting to strap on my harness. Colby is already buckled into his. "It'll be fun. I dare you to bungee jump... or are you too scared?"

I hate him. He knew he'd get me with that comment. I hate backing down from a challenge. I yank the waiver out of his hand and scribble my signature on it. One of the men who works here takes it from me and places it in the pocket of his cargo shorts before arranging my harness on the ground. I step into it, taking deep breaths... because I'm about to free-fall off the extremely tall platform above me.

Once it's buckled and deemed secure by the employees,

they tell us to go on up. Oh, yay. I glare at Colby, who's totally calm. He gives me a reassuring smile. "Ladies first."

With a groan, I grab the ladder and climb up. The metal platform is in the middle of a forest, but the surrounding area has been cleared out for safety. It's quite picturesque out here. As I climb higher and higher, I stay focused on the forest instead of how high up I am. I'm not scared of heights, but I'm scared of plunging to my death. Isn't everyone?

I step onto the platform and two more employees greet us, a woman who's brunette and probably in her forties, and a man around the same age. I allow Colby to pass by me and stay where I'm at, clinging to the pole in the center of the platform.

The woman smiles at me. "Hey guys! I'm Andrea, and this is Logan. There's nothing to be nervous about. Bungee jumping is very safe."

The blond man extends his arm to me. "You'll have so much fun, you'll be begging to go again," he teases.

Andrea looks at Colby. "Did you want to go separate, or together?"

I answer, "separate."

And at the same time Colby says, "together."

He quirks a brow. "Won't it ease your mind jumping with me instead of going alone?"

I study him intently for a moment. He's taking this seriously and is clearly not nervous at all. His hands are steady, his shoulders are set. This Colby is so different from how I usually see him. He's focused and intense. This is probably what he's like when playing hockey, too. Sure, steady, confident.

"Okay, fine," I say, letting go of the pole so they can connect us.

"Keep your arms wrapped around each other so you don't separate," Andrea explains.

Colby wastes no time stepping in close and pulling me to him. I can admit that I feel more secure with his arms around me. If this big, solid man is holding me, surely nothing bad can happen. Which is the only reason I wrap my arms around his waist and lean my face against his muscled chest.

Colby slowly rubs circles on my back with his hands, and I don't ask him to stop because it's actually helping me relax. It's also giving me a sensation I can't quite describe. Something akin to a shiver, but different.

It's probably the evening air growing cooler.

I look down at where his arms overlap my own and I notice the dark hair along his olive skin. I hadn't noticed it before, maybe because his skin is so tan that it just blends in. It's surprisingly masculine and attractive. I'm slightly annoyed that it's attractive for men to have arm hair, but gross if women do. My inner feminist prickles at the idea.

Andrea and Logan fasten and buckle the bungee cord onto our leg straps and I'm trying not to think about it. When they step back, Colby leans close and whispers, "it's okay, take a deep breath."

I exhale, my shoulders relaxing in the process.

"You guys are good to go whenever you're ready," Logan tells us.

"Are you ready, angel?" Colby whispers against my ear.

Keeping my eyes squeezed shut, I answer, "yes, okay."

After a moment, I feel Colby take a step, pulling me along with him. He falls back off the platform, holding me tightly to his chest. And I scream as we free-fall. When I finally open my eyes, I see Colby grinning and laughing, clearly loving this. We reach the end of our bungee cord, and it snaps us up and down. I finally release a laugh of my own, realizing we made it, and our bungee didn't snap and kill us.

My heart is beating rapidly from the rush of falling. It hits me that I'm wrapped in this man's arms and my face is pressed against his very solid pecs. Heat rushes to my face, and I try to lift my head off of him, but quickly think better of it. Because his strong body feels secure, whether I want to admit it or not. His muscles are also incredible, I can feel how chiseled they are through his clothing. He must work out constantly. For the first time, I wonder if this professional athlete thing is more work than I thought.

As our bouncing slows and we hang there, gently swaying from the bungee cord, Colby smiles at me. "You did amazing." He pauses, holding my gaze. I can't seem to look away, stunned by how striking his blue eyes are. It's not fair how handsome he is. "*You're* amazing."

It shouldn't make my heart swell, but it does. I mean, who doesn't like praise? I force myself to turn away from him. The sudden tension between us feels like too much, and I can't make sense of it.

I don't like this man, remember? He's annoying.

"That was pretty fun," I admit with a shrug, breaking the silence.

"Wanna do it again?" he asks, and I meet his gaze again. His eyes are twinkling with amusement.

"No."

My short answer makes him laugh again.

The guys who helped us get suited up for the jump help us down and then remove our gear. Then a group of people in business casual attire walk toward us with big smiles on their faces.

"Ah, that would be the publicity team," Colby says.

"Mr. Knight," a woman, with a blonde bob says. She shakes

Colby's hand, then turns to me and extends her hand again. "I'm Megan Barker. I'm the head of public relations for the team. Congratulations on winning an evening with an Eagle!"

She exuberantly pumps my hand, then peers at the team behind her. She introduces the three others with her. "This is Joe. He's a journalist for the Eagles. And then there's Brett. He'll be taking a few photos for our social media."

Brett waves. "I already got some great shots!"

Megan smiles and gestures to the last person. "Natalie is here to assist." Natalie smiles and I smile back.

They have two folding chairs for us to sit in, and after that jump my legs are still wobbly, and I'm thankful for the seat. Colby sits down beside me.

Joe steps closer to Colby and me. He's wearing a white button down that contrasts nicely with his dark brown skin, he looks young but acts like the professional he is. He grabs a notebook out of his satchel and a pen. "Do you guys need some more time before we get into it? I'll just ask you some fun questions for the article about the charity auction."

I take a deep breath. "No, I'm good. Ask away." My hands are still shaking slightly, but that won't affect my ability to answer questions.

"Great!" He taps his pen against his chin while he studies his notes. "What was your reaction when you won the auction?"

I snort a laugh. "I didn't win… my grandmother did."

His dark eyebrows shoot up. "Really?"

"Yep, but she made me come tonight instead." I glance at Colby, who's rolling his eyes but smirking.

Megan huffs a disbelieving laugh. "Wait a minute, you didn't want to spend an evening with Colby?"

I look at Colby again. His arms are crossed, and he's waiting for my answer with an annoying smile on his face.

"Not particularly. He's kind of annoying."

The whole team bursts into laughter. Even Colby is chuckling.

"Wow," Megan says with an amused smirk. "You might be the only person in the district that feels that way. Mr. Knight here is the darling of the NHL."

Something crashes in the background, some kind of photography lighting umbrella they had set up. Brett and Natalie are clearly struggling with the equipment.

Megan groans. "Although, he could've chosen an easier location for this." She eyes Colby. "Couldn't you have taken her ice-skating at the team's iceplex as we suggested?"

I gasp. "We could've done something as simple and not scary as ice-skating?"

"That's too boring, even for you, angel," Colby says matter-of-factly.

Joe looks between me and Colby. "Wait, did you guys already know each other before tonight?"

"Unfortunately, yes."

"She was thrilled to spend the evening with me. This is all an act," Colby says with a wink before wrapping an arm around my shoulders and pulling me against his hard torso.

I haven't dated much, and I've only kissed one man, so I'm no expert. But are men's bodies usually this firm? I'm going to research this later.

I shrug away from him. "Whatever."

The publicity team gapes at me like I'm insane, especially Natalie, the assistant who's probably midtwenties. Well, she can have him. Sure, it was comforting to have him hold me during the jump, but that was a life-and-death situation.

Brett, the photographer, has salt and pepper hair and kind blue eyes. Now that the equipment for lighting is fixed and working, he stalks toward us, a large camera in hand.

Colby smolders for the camera, really hamming it up. I can't help the smile that tugs at my lips at how over-the-top he is. He's not so bad when there's no one else around, but when he has an audience, he goes back into his annoying, arrogant mode. I can't help but wonder if it's a façade. A mask. Like he wants to keep his real-self hidden from the world, and this is the persona he adapts for the public. There might be more to Colby Knight than he shows at first glance.

"Okay, you two," Brett says. "Why don't you guys sit and talk to each other. Pretend we're not here and act natural. People want to know what an evening with Colby is like, so let's show them." He brings the camera to his face and snaps a few pictures.

"Yeah," Colby whispers in my ear. "Let's show them all how amazing I am. Now throw your head back and laugh, so everyone thinks I'm funny."

I elbow him in the ribs, obviously not hard enough, because he laughs right in my ear. He pulls away from me, giving me space. I notice again that the evening is getting chilly when his warm body is no longer in my vicinity. He's quite warm.

Another thing to research. Do men run warmer than women? I wonder if Dr. Hawthorne is this warm. How comforting it must be to curl up with a warm man every night. No wonder Andie and Mel never want to go out.

"This is great," Brett tells us, clicking through his own photos. "Eagle's fans will eat this up."

I withhold an eye roll. I still need Colby's help to ensnare Dr. Hawthorne. I need to play nice.

"How was your night with Colby?" Mel asks the following morning, taking a dainty sip of the herbal tea I prepared for her. Little non-caffeine drinking freak that she is.

She says caffeine makes her anxiety worse. I should probably try it out next time I have to be social. However, the only thing worse than being in a room full of people you don't know, is not being caffeinated.

"Night?" I raise my eyebrows. "You make it sound like I slept with him, Mel."

She giggles into her teacup, then sets it down on my coffee table. I'm happy we can still spend Saturday mornings together most weeks. After being roommates for several years, I miss having her around.

"I don't think Colby would mind if you did."

I'm sipping my hot coffee as she speaks, and her words cause me to drink too fast. I splutter and cough, making the hot liquid drip down the front of my pajamas. "Look what your perverse mind made me do! This is my favorite mumu."

Melanie throws her head back and laughs. "I can't believe you wear those nightgowns your gram keeps giving you."

"Hey now, the one perk of *not* being a newlywed is that I can still sleep in comfortable garments instead of restrictive lingerie. Leave me be."

She sighs. "You act like I'm wearing a corset to bed every night."

"Aren't you?"

She gets a mischievous glint in her eye. "West prefers when I sleep naked."

Thankfully, I don't have a mouthful of coffee this time. Otherwise, I would've spewed it across the room. "Married life has made you naughty."

We hear noise coming from the front door, and a moment

later it opens. Andie, Mitch's fiancée, enters my apartment with a smile. Her eyes flit between the two of us.

"Am I missing all the fun?" she asks before tucking the key I gave her into her purse. She's in her pajamas like me and Mel. Andie's are white shorts with smiley faces on them and a matching tee. Mel is wearing one of West's Eagles t-shirts with leggings.

"Nah," Mel says, getting up and pulling Andie into a big hug. I stand and do the same, then she sits on the sofa beside Mel, curling her legs underneath her.

"Noel was wondering if I wear a negligee to bed every night."

Andie's eyebrows raise. "And do you?"

"Not *every* night."

The three of us laugh. Getting up from the comfy chair I'm in, I walk to the kitchen and pour a mug of coffee for Andie. I fill it about one-third with caramel creamer, the way she prefers it. I think back to Colby's cinnamon roll creamer at Pancake Palace and smile to myself.

When I plop down into my seat again, Mel eyes me. "Anyway, you never answered the question. How was your evening with Colby?"

Andie settles into the couch cushions, watching me with rapt attention. "Oh yeah! That was last night, right?"

I shrug, ignoring the weird flutter in my stomach at the mention of his name. "It was fine, I guess. You guys act like I had a hot date or something."

"Girl," Andie says with a quirk of one eyebrow. "Most girls would give their left boob to spend an evening with that man."

I grab my own boobs, gaping in mock-horror. "Not me. I don't have any to spare."

"Oh stop, your boobs are fine. Tell us more about what you guys did!" Mel appears slightly exasperated at my hedging.

"Okay, he took me to Pancake Palace, and then he tricked me into bungee jumping."

They both gasp and I think it's because of the bungee jumping part, but that's not what shocked them.

"He took you to the Pancake Palace?" Mel asks.

I glance between them, confused. "Um, yeah."

Andie blows out a slow breath. "Colby's crush is more serious than I thought."

Mel nods her head dramatically. "Noel, the Pancake Palace is Colby's happy place... his sacred ground. He never takes anyone with him and won't even tell the guys which location he goes to."

A funny feeling twists my stomach, but I ignore it. "It's not a big deal. It's just some chain."

"Whatever you say," Andie says, hiding her smile behind her coffee mug. "So, how was the bungee jumping? Did you go by yourself or tandem?"

"Tandem."

They gasp again.

"Oh, my gosh. So, you two bungee jumped in each other's arms? Girl!" Andie squeals.

"I don't care what you say," Mel says. "That *was* a hot date."

I wave a hand in the air, brushing them off. "I'm interested in a guy I work with. Colby might be every other girl's type, but he's no Dúnedain." They seem confused, they must need to brush up on their Tolkien terminology.

Mel finishes her tea and I stand to get her some more, but she practically shoves me back down to a seated position. "Noel, I remember where the tea is."

Andie sighs. "It must've been fun to be roommates! Noah makes a terrible roommate." She smirks as if thinking of a memory of her much-younger brother.

"Don't worry, Andie," Mel shouts from the small kitchen. "You'll have a big, broody roommate soon enough."

Andie grins. "I can't wait. Two and a half months seems like forever."

I'm glad Mitch makes her happy. I've definitely seen a softer side of the brute since Andie and Noah came into his life, but he still terrifies me a little.

Mel walks back into the living room and takes a seat, steaming cup of tea in hand. "It's going to fly by!"

A wistful sigh escapes me before I can hold it back. The girls eye me with concern and then look at each other with a subtle grimace.

"Sorry, we didn't mean to talk about the wedding so much. I'm sure it gets annoying," Andie offers.

"Stop, I love hearing about your wedding! And about Mel's lingerie. But it does make me want that for myself too, you know? I'm beyond happy for you guys. Sometimes it reminds me I'm nearing thirty and don't even have a boyfriend." I offer a small smile and they smile back.

"Tell us about this Dr. Hawthorne," Mel says, leaning forward in her seat.

Andie does the same. "Ohh, he sounds classy."

I lean forward too, resting my elbows on my knees and clasping my hands together. "He is. *And* he's British."

CHAPTER 11
COLBY

SUNDAY, I get together with the guys for a workout in Remy's home gym. The best part, it's not a far commute considering I live in the same cul-de-sac. If only West, Mitch, and Bruce would move over here too it would be a whole party.

There's a large room right behind Remy's garage that he transformed into a state-of-the-art gym, with all the newest and best gym equipment. Two walls are lined with mirrors, but besides that there's no decor, or colorful paint. Which matches the rest of Remy's house. Black and white.

Bruce, Remy, and I have worked out together at least once a week in the off season for years. West joined us when he got traded to the Eagles a little more than a year ago. And it's just been recently that Mitch started working out with us too. Mitch used to keep to himself completely, only speaking to any of us if he was pissed off. But he's changed a lot since meeting Andie and going to counseling with the team therapist. Still, he's grumbling that Andie made him come today. Apparently, she told him it's good for him to socialize and get a break from her and Noah.

Preseason starts this week. Which means this might be our last home-gym sesh together for a while. With the chaos of our NHL workouts and game schedule.

We're hitting it hard today. Preseason might be the time for the newbies to shine, but us veteran players need to be honed and ready too.

We're halfway through our first set of deadlifts when my brain flits back to thoughts of a certain curly-headed blonde. A woman who at first glance is sweet and angelic, but whose bite could rival a cobra. I smile to myself. That woman. "I need your help winning Noel over," I blurt it out a little too loud and they all stare at me.

West puts his barbell down and studies me seriously. "I knew this conversation was coming when Mel told me you took her to Pancake Palace."

"Yeah," I nod. "It's serious."

"Wow, really man? I feel hurt," Bruce adds, swiping at his sweaty forehead with the back of his hand.

"Maybe someday I'll take you Bruce," I say, but we both know I'm lying.

Remy eyes me thoughtfully, always the introspective one. "I have to ask, what is it about Noel that makes you suddenly so… into commitment?"

Bruce and West snicker.

"If Mitch can be marriageable, I can too!" I glance at Mitch. "No offense."

Mitch shrugs. "None taken. Commitments aren't so bad when you meet *the one*."

Remy places his hands on his hips. "How do you know she's the one you want, Colby?"

All four of them whip their heads to stare at me, waiting to hear what I have to say.

"Well, obviously she's gorgeous."

Bruce scoffs. "Obviously."

I glare at him, and he shuts up.

I continue, holding up one finger as I count off her best attributes. "One... She's smart, like really freaking smart. I need to marry someone with a high IQ to make up for my lack of one."

Remy rolls his eyes, but Mitch nods, agreeing with me.

"Two, she'd rather curl up and read a book than go out to a club. Homebodies are incredibly underrated. You know how many girls want me to parade them around so they can be seen with me? No one ever wants to spend a date cuddling with me on the sofa, watching a movie."

They all mutter their agreements, seeing my point.

"Three, she puts me in my place when I'm being an ass. She's not afraid to speak her mind."

"You like that?" Bruce asks, arching a brow.

"I like it when *she* does it. Don't get any ideas."

Ignoring his laughter, I continue, "four, she's close to her family. I just found this one out a few nights ago. But I love that."

"Five, she's loyal. Have you seen her around Mel and Andie? That woman would go to war for them. If someone messes with her friends, she'll morph into a feral bobcat before you can snap your fingers."

They all laugh at that, but I know they see it. Even Mitch has a knowing smirk on his face.

West looks at me with a hesitant smile, he's the only one I've talked to about my dad's history. He knows how important loyalty is to me.

I hold up a sixth finger, but West stops me, holding his hands out in front of him. "Okay, okay. We get it. So, how can we help?"

I scratch the back of my head. "That's the thing. I don't

know… I've never done this before. I'm usually the one being chased."

"Hashtag humble brag," Bruce singsongs.

"I know, it makes me sound like a tool. But it's the truth, and if we're honest, it's been that way for all of us. Don't act like I'm the only one."

Mitch scoffs. "Maybe. But you *are* the prettiest, and you know it."

I pretend to flip imaginary long-hair over my shoulder. "Don't hate me for what my mama gave me."

"Speaking of your mom, she still single?" Bruce waggles his eyebrows. The man has a thing for older women. I'm not sure I've ever seen him date someone his own age.

"Shut up! She's a married woman now," I proudly puff my chest out. "Anyway," I say. "I need to know how to pursue a woman, how to make her fall in love with me. And we have at least two experts right in this room."

West and Mitch grin. Not sure I've ever seen Mitch smile this big. But he's a happily engaged man, after all.

"And another thing, she told me there's this professor she's into. She wants me to teach her how to get his attention." I look down at my feet. It's embarrassing to admit.

The guys wear matching grimaces.

"Dang," Remy says. "That's rough. This is going to be a challenge for sure."

"Yeah," I admit. "But I thought it would at least force her to talk to me, and maybe even go on some practice dates."

Bruce chuckles. "That's brilliant. Use the dating lessons, or whatever you want to call it, to win her heart and show her how much you want her."

"Exactly." I smile.

I drag a hand through my hair, remembering our conversation at Pancake Palace. "And it pisses me off that this guy made her think she needs to change. He must be the biggest idiot alive."

"Noel's going to a fantasy convention this coming weekend," Mitch says, and we all stare at him, shocked he's adding to the conversation. "What?" He throws his hands up. "Andie told me." He shrugs. "What if you showed up at the convention, dressed up and everything? Show her you care about her interests."

West and Bruce slap Mitch on the back with good-natured pats.

"That's perfect," West says. "She's taking her little sister too. Win over the sister and you might earn Noel's approval too."

I pat my athletic shorts and shirtless chest as if searching for a pen and paper. Bruce holds one finger up like he has an idea, then grabs a dry erase marker from the floor that Remy used to write out our workout.

Bruce pulls the cap off and writes, in huge, sloppy letters, *becoming Noel's Knight in shining armor.* Beneath that he writes:

1. Fantasy convention, show her you know and enjoy her interests.

Remy stares at the messy mirror with a horrified expression and I wonder if he's going to clean it spotless with Windex the moment we all leave.

West grabs the marker from Bruce and adds a number two under the first item on the list. He continues writing, and when he pulls back, we read what he wrote.

2. Show Noel she's perfect the way she is, and she doesn't need to change for Dr. Dickhead.

We laugh as we read his handwriting, which is just as unkempt as Bruce's. Except Remy, his eyes are still wide, staring at the mirror.

Mitch grabs the marker next, surprising all of us. He hunches as he writes, and Bruce reads it aloud,

"3. Read all of Noel's favorite books."

He elbows Mitch playfully. "Mitch 'The Machine,' You're good at this!"

Mitch shrugs off the compliment.

With a heavy sigh, Remy finally joins the fun and grabs the marker. He adds a number four to the list and writes:

4. *Show her she's the only girl you have eyes for. Don't touch, or even look, at another woman.*

"I know this one seems obvious. But with your past escapades, I'd imagine it would be extra important to gain Noel's trust," he says seriously, looking straight into my eyes for a beat too long.

The intense eye contact and the no-nonsense expression is terrifying. I gulp. "Yes, sir." Remy keeps writing.

5. *Earn Noel's trust.*

West breaks the tension by yanking the marker out of his hand. "I have one more!" He then proceeds to write a number six:

6. *Win over her family, win over the girl.*

Bruce holds his hand out for the marker, and I withhold an eye roll. This list is getting long, but I did *ask* for their help. Bruce pauses with the marker close to the mirror then taps it against his strong, dimpled chin. "Would you say you're a good kisser?"

My head jerks back and I gasp. "Of course, I am!"

Bruce wags his index finger at me. "Not just a good kisser. Anyone, including Dr. Dickhead, could be a good kisser. I need to know if you're an epic, once in a lifetime kind of kisser."

West takes a step closer to me, studying my mouth. "I bet he is, he has the right lips."

Remy's eyebrows draw together as he studies me. "I think you're right. The perfect amount of pout."

Mitch quirks a brow. "But does he know what to do with his tongue?"

My face twists up. "You are *not* asking me about tongue action."

Mitch's face is flat, void of emotion. "Some guys don't know what to do with their tongues while kissing. Andie told me some horror stories."

West clears his throat. "But do you have a tongue tie? That can be an issue too. Mel dated some guy named Jeff who had a tongue tie. Horrible experience."

"My tongue is fine," I say with a groan. "Perfect actually."

Bruce tips his chin in a serious nod, then writes on the mirror:

7. Give Noel a kiss she can't forget. Tasteful amount of tongue included.

———

The next day, I arrive back home from an early morning practice with the team. I already showered in the locker room at the Eagles' iceplex, so I strip down to my boxer briefs and settle in my big bed for a long nap. With a tired sigh, I pick up The Hobbit from my nightstand, and open it up. I'm on chapter five and I'm hoping to finish another chapter before drifting off, but first, I snap a pic of myself holding it and send it to Noel.

I'm pleasantly surprised when she texts right back.

NOEL

Seriously? Now I'm getting selfies of you in bed?

I laugh, letting my head fall back against my wood headboard, then look down at myself. I'm covered from the waist down with my navy bedspread. But it totally appears like I'm nude in the photo.

COLBY

I notice you focused on me in bed... but didn't even notice I'm holding a book.

NOEL

I noticed the book!

COLBY

Riiiiiiiiiight. *wink emoji*

NOEL

You give me a headache. Hope you're enjoying the book.

COLBY

Enjoying it so far. Although, the author is a little wordy.

NOEL

Professor Tolkien is a master with words! He was a philologist, after all. Have YOU done anything as cool as inventing multiple languages? I think not. Trust the process.

COLBY

Okay, fine. I'll keep reading. Have a great day, Angel. *blowing kiss emoji*

I wake up from my nap, my book splayed across my chest. Blinking the sleep out of my eyes, I replace my bookmark and lay *The Hobbit* back on the nightstand. Apparently, I fell asleep reading again.

With a loud yawn, I stretch and get up and out of bed, scratching my stomach where the pages left little marks on my skin. I walk down the hallway that leads from my bedroom to the kitchen. My bare feet are cold against the tile, and it hits me that this big house is starting to feel more quiet and lonelier the longer I live here. It's eerily quiet, there's a ringing in my ears, as if my ears are trying to create noise for me to listen to. I used to be out on the town all the time, hardly ever home. But I don't have the desire to go out all the time anymore. And finding some random hookup doesn't interest me anymore. I'm kind of disappointed it ever did. Disappointed in that small piece of me that's just like my dad.

I bought this house years ago simply because it's in the same neighborhood as Remy. But I've never known what to do with all the extra space. I suppose it's time to hire a designer or something. There's a whole upstairs that I completely forget about, with gorgeous, vaulted ceilings, and distressed wood beams. It's all wasted on a bachelor with no design intuition.

Grabbing the empty coffee pot from the coffee maker, I pad to the sink to fill it up, when I hear my phone ring. I run back to my room where I left my phone and see my dad is calling. Reluctantly, I answer it.

"Hey, Dad."

His booming voice comes from the speaker. "How's my favorite son?"

I sigh and shift on my feet. I'm his only son... that we know of. "Doing okay, what's up?"

"Can't I call to chat and catch up with my boy?"

I arch a brow even though he can't see me. My dad has never called just to chat. "Sure, you can. How are you?"

He hedges. "Well, actually, there is a reason for my call."

I snort an unamused laugh and he continues. "Serenity wants to take a trip into the city. Didn't know if we could stay with you in that big, fancy house of yours?"

"Is Ruthie coming?" I ask a little too excitedly. I'll gladly put up with my dad and his girlfriend if I get to see my baby sister.

Dad groans. "Unfortunately, yes. We couldn't find a sitter."

I grit my teeth. My dad and his ungrateful attitude always seem to draw my prickly side to the surface. Me and Ma weren't enough for him, I know. But now he has an amazing little girl, the cutest kid ever, and he's still not happy. Serenity is okay too, I guess. I wrinkle my nose at the thought of my dad's girlfriend, who's five years younger than me.

"You know you're always welcome to come visit, Dad. But preseason is starting, and I might not be around much." I take a seat on the edge of my bed, running a hand through my hair. The thought of my dad staying here always stresses me out... he's so... difficult to please. "When are you thinking of coming?"

Dad blows out a long breath. "Serenity scheduled a spa day for Saturday."

I rub my temples with my free hand. "Saturday, as in this Saturday?"

"I know it's impromptu, but what with all the hockey games I drove you to, and equipment I purchased over the years, I didn't think it would be a big deal."

I want to remind him that Ma is the one who drove me to all those practices and games. He might've written a child-support check, but she's the one who made sure I had all the best gear and signed me up for the training camps that would grow my skills. Meanwhile, he was running around with his flavor of the week.

"Right," I say through gritted teeth. I put up with this man only so I can have a relationship with my sister. The thought of her dark, curly head and deep dimples instantly brings a smile to my face. She's my mini me... which means a miniature of my father as well. I keep hoping he'll get pudgy and go bald, but he keeps getting more handsome and distinguished with age. The bastard.

Good news for my future, though, I suppose.

"Perfect!" he says loudly, making me pull my phone away from my ear with a grimace. "We'll see you Saturday morning and will head back to Virginia on Monday."

"Okay," I say, the gold-foiled edges of *The Hobbit* catch my eye and I remember the fantasy convention this weekend. "Oh, I have plans on Saturday already, but should be home for dinner."

I hear a low, devilish laugh come from the speaker. "Do we need to leave the house that day? You bringing some girls over?"

I roll my eyes. Aggravated at his question. Aggravated with him, and a little at myself too. Because a year ago, I probably would've been bringing girls back here.

"No, Dad. I'm going to a convention."

"Sounds good, son. I'll have Serenity prepare her famous tofu salad for dinner that night. As a thank you for letting us stay with you."

I gag involuntarily. Serenity is a horrible cook... and tofu? No thanks. "Wow, really generous of you guys. See you Saturday."

CHAPTER 12
NOEL

MONDAY AND TUESDAY I didn't hear from Colby. I could tell he was hesitant about the whole dating coach thing... but I need his help. I think the preseason started, so I was trying to be patient.

It's Wednesday morning now, and still nothing. I'm getting my morning coffee in the campus coffee shop, when the bell above the door chimes and Dr. Hawthorne strides inside. I panic. Colby hasn't given me any instructions yet, and I always make a fool of myself in front of this man. Ducking into the small bathroom before he can see me, I slam the door and lock it.

"Oh no," I mutter. "I forgot my coffee." With a groan, I dig inside my purse and pull my phone out. Staring at the screen for a second, I tap on the contact of the last person I want to talk to, but the only one who can help me. The phone rings three times before Colby's gravely, sleepy voice answers. My heart beats faster at his just-woke-up voice and I refuse to delve into the reason why. Not when I'm in the middle of a Dexter-mergency.

"Good morning, angel," he purrs. "Is this a booty call? I knew you'd cave, eventually."

"Would you be serious?" I yell through the phone. "I need your help!"

He groans. "Okay, okay. But you woke me up at eight thirty in the morning on the *one* day I get to sleep in this week."

"You'll survive. Anyway, I'm in the campus coffee shop, and Dr. Hawthorne walked inside! I panicked!"

I hear him blow out a slow breath. "Alright, relax. What's the problem, exactly?"

"You haven't given me any instructions yet! I don't know how to talk to him!"

"Where are you? Are you still in the coffee shop?"

"Yes, I'm hiding in the bathroom."

"Lesson number one," he says with humor in his voice, like he's desperately trying not to laugh. "Don't hide from the person you're trying to get to notice you."

"Very funny." I put my back to the door and lean against it. "Every time I talk to him, I say something stupid. He never even smiles at me."

"He's a stoic Brit, Noel." His voice sounds annoyed, and I think this is the first time he's used my real name. Maybe he isn't a morning person? "Any guy would be flattered to have a beautiful woman trip all over themselves trying to talk to him, okay? There's no way he hasn't noticed. Go be yourself. Even if you're dorky or say something stupid. The first lesson of flirtation is confidence."

I'm momentarily stunned. He referred to me as beautiful. Now, if I was a good feminist, my heart wouldn't flutter at the compliment. But apparently, I'm not a good feminist.

"Confidence?" I squeak out, suddenly feeling more nervous, and hotter.

"Fake it til you make it."

With a deep breath I thank him, and we end the call. I hope Colby falls back asleep, because he was a real bear about this conversation.

I open the bathroom door, straightening my spine, and step out into the coffee shop. I'm feigning confidence and taking a few runway-worthy steps before glancing around the room. Dexter is near the coffee bar, lounging against the wall with his ankles crossed. The pose has the hem of his trousers pulled up enough that I can see he's wearing green and blue argyle socks, which pair nicely with his navy sweater-vest.

The young barista holds up a travel cup, reading what's written on the side, "Plain, black coffee?"

"That's me," Dexter says proudly, his nose always tilted toward the ceiling.

The young man appears bored and hands him the cup before rushing back for another order. I spot my own coffee, a hazelnut, butter latte, waiting for me on the counter and take a step forward. When Dexter turns to leave, he spots me. And to my delight, his face absolutely lights up upon seeing me. I'm sure my expression matches him, since I'm delighted that he's delighted. Maybe I didn't freak him out at all. Maybe he's into smart, awkward girls who word-vomit their every thought.

"Dr. Woodcock, I was hoping to run into you."

"You were?" I say way too quickly and a much too loud. I clear my throat and try again. "Well, here I am."

His next words make me deflate faster than a balloon on a hot, summer's day. "I didn't realize you're friends with Colby Knight. I saw the Eagles' article on you two. I'm a big fan, being an athlete myself and all."

He. Did. Not.

I force a laugh, and it definitely *sounds* forced. "Oh. Yeah. My best friend is married to Weston Kershaw, it's no big deal."

His jaw drops. "You know the entire team?"

Oops. I should've just left it at Colby. "I mean, I don't *know* them."

"But I saw photographs of you and Colby Knight having a bit of fun, you even bungee jumped together."

I close my eyes and count to two. "It was a thing for charity. My Grandmother made me go in her place."

He laughs, looking unconvinced. "You didn't want to spend an evening with *the* Colby Knight?"

I shrug. "He's not really my type."

He looks down at his sweater vest, snickering to himself. "Love, he's every girl's type."

My heartbeat quickens at the term of endearment. *Love.* It sounds divine coming from his British lips. "Not mine," I say, my voice coming out all breathy. I swallow and square my shoulders, remembering what Colby said about confidence. My eyes dip down his torso, taking in his lean, narrow waist— accentuated by the vest—then back up to his face.

One of his perfectly shaped blond brows arches slowly. "So," he says slowly. "You're not *with* Colby?"

"No, of course not," I say defensively.

He smiles at me, it's a sexy, salacious smile. Then says, "Duly noted." Then he raises his plain, black coffee toward me and strides out of the coffee shop.

And they say women are confusing. I was pretty clear, and he's toying with me. But he was flirting! I'm almost sure of it. My Colby lessons are already working.

I type out a text, practically giddy.

NOEL

It worked! OMG. He definitely flirted with me.

He never responds.

CHAPTER 13
COLBY

"IT'S NOT WORKING!" I throw my hands up in frustration after our afternoon practice. The guys have lockers near mine, and they all lean in to listen.

"I told her to be confident, even if she ends up being dorky, and then he flirted with her! Flirted! How am I supposed to compete with a British accent?"

"To be clear," Mitch says, swiping his brow with a towel. "You're talking about Dr. Dickhead?"

"Obviously! Try to keep up."

West and Bruce grimace and give each other a Colby-has-gone-mad look.

Remy, always level-headed and wise, offers, "you're a wealthy professional athlete, you live in a mansion. And according to Sports Illustrated, last year you were the sexiest athlete of the year."

I bang my head against the frame of my polished wooden cubby, it's the fancy version of a locker. "That was last year. This year the award goes to Dr. Hawthorne. Who's also an athlete, apparently." I remember Noel telling me he went to Uni on a pickleball scholarship and start laughing maniacally.

"He's an athlete?" Bruce asks.

West folds his arms over his chest. "What does he play?"

I'm still laughing, but manage to squeak out, "pickleball."

Mitch rolls his eyes. "Oh wow, yeah. He's some fierce competition indeed."

My laughter turns into a groan. "And he wears sweater vests, which is Noel's crack."

Remy's face scrunches. "Your girl is a freak."

West laughs. "That's some grandpa bullshit right there. Sweaters and pickleball."

"Right? I'm surprised she's not married to an eighty-year-old man."

I rip my elbow pads off and throw them into my cubby.

West takes a seat on the bench, growing serious. "What if Dr. what's-his-face falls in love with her and sweeps her off her feet? If he's the guy who truly made her happy, would you bow out?"

I slump down beside him, my pads forgotten. "It would hurt, but yes. I'd always remove my shirt when I was around them though. Gotta remind her what she missed out on."

All four of them throw their sweaty pads at my face and I bring my arms up to block them.

"I wouldn't give up yet, Colby," Remy says, patting me on the back. "He flirted with her, so what? I've seen you play your heart out on the ice, and I know you'll fight for Noel with that same determination."

"Yeah, man. You got this," West adds. "What are you dressing up as for the fantasy convention?"

I rub my hands together. "Oh, I have the perfect costume. And my baby sister will be here to help me pull it off."

"Your parents are visiting? The first week of preseason?" Mitch asks, as if annoyed for me.

"My dad and his girlfriend, yes. And I know. But they tell

me when they're coming, without ever asking if it's a good time for me."

"Ahh, the vegan?" West feigns a gag.

"The one and only. And she's making me her famous vegan casserole, so you're all welcome to come over Saturday night." I sit down beside West and remove my shin pads.

Mitch and West start moaning and pretending to throw up.

"Sorry, I'll be too busy clipping my toenails," Bruce teases.

"I'd come, but the commute is too far. You know how traffic is around here." Remy's voice is so serious when he says it, but he has that twinkle of sarcasm in his eye that only people who know him would notice.

"Yeah, that ten-foot walk is brutal."

———

When I arrive home from practice, I text Noel. I feel guilty for not responding to her text earlier. But I don't even want to think about another man flirting with her. I want her to flirt with me and only me. I'm a selfish pig, this is no surprise to anyone.

I need to make this stubborn woman see how good we could be together. I know there's something under the surface that she's refusing to believe. An undeniable attraction that could easily turn into more. And if I'm going to show her how much better I am for her than Dr. Dickhead, then I need to spend more time with her.

COLBY

I think we should go on a fake date. You obviously need practice.

I smile when she responds right away.

NOEL

A fake date? Is this a ploy?

COLBY

Just trying to help. That's what you asked me for, right?

NOEL

Okay. It couldn't hurt.

COLBY

Tomorrow night we have a preseason game, but how about the next evening?

NOEL

I'm free that night.

COLBY

Great. You have to act like this is a real date, dress up and everything. And I'm going to pick you up.

NOEL

eyeroll emoji we don't need to take it that seriously.

COLBY

Yes, we do. Making conversation in the car on the way to the restaurant is the worst part of the whole date. Therefore, you need to practice.

NOEL

Okay fine. You have a point.

I pump my fist into the air. "I have a date with Noel!" I shout to my empty house. Even though she thinks it's fake, it's progress.

Pulling up to Noel's apartment complex Friday evening, I take a moment to study my surroundings. To picture her here, parking her Chevy Bel Air, shuffling through her purse. Stepping inside her apartment that I just know is cozy… toeing off her shoes and curling up with a book. I want to be there for all of it. I want to watch her in every simple moment of life, see her graceful movements and be part of them. To embrace her in the kitchen while she cooks, to sit on the couch and read together at night. To go to bed with her, kissing up and down her body, then waking up tangled together.

She makes me want things I didn't ever think I could want. I thought I'd be like my dad, playing around forever. Taking advantage of the attention women give me. But I look at my mother, who's waited years to meet that perfect guy. The one who will love her forever. And then I see my father, who dated anything with a pulse, until one got pregnant. And even then, it's only a matter of time before he leaves Serenity for a new pursuit. And little Ruthie will be left in the wake of his selfishness. A pattern I'm all too familiar with. Except she has a big brother who will always keep an eye on her, always love her.

Even the dread of seeing my dad and Serenity this weekend is overshadowed by the joy of seeing Ruthie. I can't wait for Noel to meet her since Ruthie is coming with me to the fantasy convention. Our costumes are going to blow her away.

Straightening my shoulders, I brush thoughts of my dad out of my head and make my way to Noel's apartment on the third floor. It's an old building, charming but slightly run down. I smile to myself, wondering if that's what drew Noel to this place. Noel, the beautiful angel with an ancient soul.

I'm about to knock on Noel's door when I feel like I'm being watched. I swivel my head to look at the door behind me, which is open just a crack, and it slams shut. Noel's door flies open, and she drags me into her apartment, muttering something under her breath that sounds like, "hurry up before Steve sees you."

A four-letter word flies out of my mouth before I can stop it and Noel glares at me with her arms crossed.

"What?" I throw my hands up. "You drag me inside your apartment with a comment about someone named Steve and expect me to stay calm?"

She relaxes, as if realizing how ridiculous the last ten seconds were. "Okay, good point. Steve is my nosey neighbor; he's retired and has nothing to do all day. And, unfortunately, he's a big Eagles fan. I don't want him inviting himself over here."

I study her apartment while she rattles on about Steve. It's similar to how I pictured it. The living room has a loveseat and two comfy-looking chairs across from it, and in place of a coffee table she has a tufted, floral ottoman. There are book-shelves all around the room. A round dining table rests on the opposite side of the living space, and there's a small kitchen right off of the dining room. It's clean, but messy and disor-derly, which surprises me. I assumed Noel was a neat freak. But the apartment looks lived-in and comfortable, like you could kick your shoes off and take a nap on the couch without messing anything up.

I realize she's paused in her rant about her neighbor, waiting for me to say something. "Very creepy," I tell her, and she seems satisfied with that.

"You have no idea. When West used to come here to see Mel, Steve would come up with the weirdest excuses to knock on our door. One time, he asked if he could borrow a cup of water, saying he had run out."

I laugh at that. "Steve isn't very creative."

"Definitely not," she says, turning and grabbing a brown,

leather purse from the small table. She's wearing navy tights with a cream-colored dress that has one of those old-fashioned collars at the neck. She's paired a dark red cardigan over the top, probably a good idea this late in September. She looks like she belongs in an old movie set somewhere in Europe.

"You look lovely."

She turns toward me, adjusting the strap of her purse on her shoulder. "Oh, thanks." She takes a moment to take in my appearance for the first time and her jaw tenses. "Really, Colby?" she asks, narrowing her eyes at my vest.

I smooth my hands down my red, cable-knit sweater vest, feigning confusion. "What? You don't like my outfit?"

"You're a pig. I'm never telling you anything ever again."

"So dramatic. I only wanted to impress you, angel." I wink at her.

Noel groans. "Let's go and get this over with."

I wag my index finger at her. "Nuh-uh-uh. Lesson number 2. Always compliment what your date is wearing." I rest my hands on my hips and tap my foot. "Go ahead, I'm waiting."

Her jaw is clenched so hard, I'm surprised her perfect teeth are still intact. She closes her eyes like she's trying to calm her temper, then opens them and gives me the fakest smile I've ever seen. "Your vest is quite dashing, Colby." She pauses then mutters, "It's a snug fit, but—"

"Thank you for noticing. I've been working out so much, my pecs are stretching the wool to its max capacity. Time to go vest shopping soon, I think."

Staring up at the ceiling, she sighs heavily. "Are you ready to go?"

"Yes, especially now that you boosted my confidence."

She slowly cracks the door and peeks at the door across the hall. "Okay, the coast is clear. Make a run for it until you get to the end of the hallway."

CHAPTER 14
NOEL

DID Colby *have* to ruin sweater vests for me? It's not that it looks bad, that's the problem. The problem is: no one could possibly look as good in a vest as Colby Knight. It's annoying. First suits, now vests? Is there any style the man can't pull off?

As a former gangly, self-conscious individual who was ridiculed by people like Colby, it infuriates me more than it should. I've learned how to dress my slight frame, and learned what a difference good posture makes, but deep inside... I'm still that scrawny, awkward college freshman.

We arrive in front of Colby's glossy, black G-Wagon and he holds the passenger door open for me. I love this car. I want to run my hand along the smooth, polished surface. If I could've afforded one, this is what I would've purchased instead of mine. Not that I don't love my classic Bel Aire. But a G-Wagon? So chic.

Once we're buckled in and on our way to wherever Colby is taking me, likely another buffet, he dives into conversation seamlessly. I realize it's actually nice to have someone else carry the conversation, to not have to stress about awkward silences.

"I'm really enjoying *The Hobbit*, I'm not finished yet, though. Once preseason started, free time stopped." He chuckles. "But I'm excited to finish it and see what happens. I think my favorite part so far was when the dwarves crashed at Bilbo's house."

"Oh yes, and how Gandalf didn't warn him?" I laugh, angling in my seat to get a better look at him. "Do you think you'll read The Lord of the Rings next?" My voice comes out a little too loud and excited.

He grins at me, not bothered by my nerdiness whatsoever. "Oh, definitely. I'm committed now."

I wonder briefly if Dexter is a Tolkien fan. I've never heard him reference Professor Tolkien's writing, but my mind usually goes blank with nerves whenever he's talking to me. Why can't conversation with Dexter be as easy as it is with Colby? I thought Colby's chattiness would be aggravating, but it's not. It's the opposite. I study him while he drives. The car is momentarily silent, but it's not awkward. Colby's profile is strong and angular, as is the rest of him. But there's also a softness about him. I'm not sure if it's those blue eyes that seem to know exactly what I'm thinking, or if it's his easy-going manner. Something tells me he'd be a great cuddler.

Whoa, Noel. Don't let that chiseled jaw get you thinking about cuddling. This man is dangerous. He's probably had five-thousand girlfriends. Not had, *has*. Colby Knight is a total playboy, and it's this whole façade that gets him all the girls.

It's the sweater-vest. It's doing weird things to me. Cuddling with Colby. Psh. I laugh to myself.

"What are you laughing about?" Colby has a relaxed smile on his face as he drives through D.C. traffic.

I clear my throat. "Nothing. When does your regular season begin? I'm sure you're excited for all the traveling and philandering."

"Philandering?" He side-eyes me before focusing on the road again.

"Yeah, partying, meeting women. Isn't that what you live for?" I'm being judgmental, I know. But everyone in D.C. is aware of Colby's reputation. He hasn't exactly hidden his escapades.

His jaw ticks. I'm not sure if he's annoyed, or uncomfortable that I brought it up. "In the past, that *is* what I lived for. But I'm not interested in that lifestyle anymore."

"Really? Why the sudden change of heart?" I'm genuinely curious.

Colby huffs a laugh. "Noel, I realize you probably don't stalk me online, but if you did, you'd know I haven't dated at all for the last year."

"A year?" My voice comes out all high-pitched and squeaky.

"You're one to talk," he teases.

"Touché."

Colby opens his mouth to speak, then snaps it shut. His expression turns thoughtful, as if thinking about what he wants to say next. "Growing up, I thought healthy relationships were non-existent. I never wanted to settle down, or risk going through a divorce like my parents." His hands tighten on the steering wheel. "But I was wrong. I've watched my mother fall in love again, and now my teammates too. And they're all better for it, better because of their partner. That's what I want too. Not random flings with women I'll never see again. That life seems pointless to me now."

I swallow, suddenly feeling like a major dirt-bag. "Wow. That's actually really sweet. Sorry for misjudging you."

He dips his chin, acknowledging my words. "It's okay, you weren't wrong, necessarily. And for the record, I never led anyone on... they were aware I wasn't a relationship guy."

I hold my hands up. "You don't have to explain. I have nothing against consensual... relationships."

Colby laughs, but it's not his usual, comfortable laugh. "Anyway," he starts.

"Yes, subject change, please."

"Does talking about sex make you uncomfortable, Noel?" He stops at a red light and peers over at me, waiting expectantly for my answer.

My cheeks are on fire. Yes, in fact, talking about sex with Colby Knight does make me uncomfortable. Not that I'm thinking about having sex *with* Colby. "Of course not." My voice comes out a little higher than usual. "We're both adults here."

He smiles, the big one, the one that makes his dimples look magnificent and lights up his whole face. "It's fun to see you squirm."

Thankfully, I'm saved from anymore sex talk as we pull up to the valet in front of The Parthenon. I try to stay calm, but this is the fanciest restaurant in D.C. One of those places that has a six month wait list.

The front of the historic, downtown building has been painted and freshened up with crisp, white paint. But still has that colonial charm from the carvings in the wood above the building and the gold sconces lining both sides of the glass doors. I watch as the elegant patrons sway into the restaurant with their designer clothes and shoes and feel instantly out of place. I know I'm blushing again. But this time with nerves. I close my eyes and take a deep breath. The warmth of a hand touching mine pulls me from my thoughts. I glance up to see Colby standing there with my door opened. I hadn't realized he'd gotten out of the vehicle and come around to my side already.

"Everything okay?" he asks, his eyebrows knitting

together. His hand covering mine is large and warm, and surprisingly comforting.

"Yeah, I'm good." I step out of the vehicle, and he doesn't let go of my hand.

Colby tucks my hand through his arm before leading me inside the restaurant and up to the ornate hostess stand.

"Mr. Knight?" The hostess says upon seeing us.

He turns to her. "Yeah, that's me."

"Right this way," the hostess says, leading us down a quiet hallway lit with the same gold wall sconces that line the walls outside. She brings us to a private table in the corner of the large restaurant. We're not completely separated from the other patrons, but enough that it's quiet, romantic even. If this was a real date, anyway.

The cozy round table has a flickering candle in the center and a classic white tablecloth. There are two leather armchairs tucked into the table. When the waiter, a young man with well-groomed black hair, appears and introduces himself as Pierre, the hostess excuses herself and heads back in the direction we just came from. Pierre walks over and pulls my chair out; I take a seat and he places my napkin in my lap for me. Colby chuckles at the surprised expression on my face. I've never been to a place so fancy that they put the napkin on your lap, I didn't even know that was a thing.

He pulls Colby's chair out next and gives him the special-napkin-treatment. We order our drinks, Colby just gets water, and I ask for a glass of wine, hoping to calm what's left of my nerves.

Once Pierre leaves us, Colby turns to me. "If your napkin shifts, I can help put it back on your lap."

I roll my eyes but am secretly glad he's back to acting like his normal, obnoxious self. A trait I'm finding more endearing and less annoying as of late. But I'll never tell Colby that.

"You act nervous," Colby comments, eyeing my fingers that are tapping on the table.

I blow out a deep breath. "I feel out of place." I look down at my hand, removing it from the table and resting it on my lap instead.

"You're only out of place here because you're not stuffy and pretentious like everyone else," he whispers, his face breaking into an easy smile. "If you were that way, I wouldn't want to spend the evening with you."

His words make my skin tingle. He's talking about tonight almost as if it's a real date. And the way he said *spending the evening with you* sounded sultry coming from his lips.

Thankfully, Pierre interrupts the charged moment. He sets our drinks down along with two of the prettiest menus I've ever seen. The covers are leather like our chairs, but the inside is white linen with gold embossed letters.

"I knew you'd love the menus," Colby muses, clearly watching me take everything in.

"This whole place is so pretty." I look around, taking in the old, plaster walls and hardwood floors, the floral arrangements and the fireplace, the lighting and the music. Everything comes together for the perfect ambiance.

"Romantic, huh?" He moves his dark eyebrows up and down.

"It really is. I'm going to be a dating expert after your coaching."

Something flashes across his face, but it's gone so quickly, I can't name what it was. He plasters his winning smile on his face and peruses his menu.

"Just water tonight?" I ask, taking a sip of my wine.

He groans. "Yeah, I know. Water is so boring. But I don't drink much during the season. I have to keep up with the youngsters."

"Is that challenging?"

He scoffs. "I mean, I'm still fast. But there's always someone younger, faster, and more talented. And now that I'm thirty, the pressure is on."

"But that's so young." I study him. He doesn't have a single grey hair among his dark ones.

"Thirty is young in most things, but not in hockey." He brings one arm up and flexes it. "But don't you worry your pretty little head. I'm staying on top of my game."

"Tell me more about your parents," I say, remembering him touching on their divorce on the drive here. I'm curious why he doesn't say much on the topic. It must not be something he talks about often.

He blows out a dramatic breath. "Another important lesson; don't ask about parents on a first date."

I roll my eyes. "But this is our second not-real-date. So, it's fine."

He tilts his head back and forth as if he's contemplating it. "I think this is more like fifth date conversation."

"Well, since we won't be going on a fifth date, we should probably squeeze all the lessons into tonight."

He groans. "Didn't realize you were such a rule-breaker, Dr. Woodcock."

I tap my fingers on the table.

"Fine." He slumps back in his chair. "My dad left me and my mother. Said he was too young to settle down, needed to experience life while he was young. And experience he did. With who knows how many women until his current girl-friend got pregnant. Hence my little sister. He's still with Serenity, but he'll get bored soon."

"Wow, that must've been hard for you and your mom."

"It sucked," he says honestly. "Watching my mother cry

over him for years made me never want to be in a relationship. Falling in love seemed horrible. Dangerous."

"But you changed your mind?"

He shoots me a half-smile. "It was impossible not to after watching Ma and my new stepdad, Charlie. He loves her the way she deserves. He's so good to her. And how could I not want what they have? Or what West and Mel have, and Mitch and Andie? Mitch fell in love and now I actually enjoy being around him. And on the opposite end of the love spectrum, I've seen my dad leave a trail of broken hearts. I don't want to be like that. The women I've been with always knew what they were getting into, but they often changed their minds. I've hurt people, not intentionally, but still." Colby's mouth turns down slightly and he studies his menu. He looks genuinely dismayed that he's hurt people.

Trying to soften the mood, I say, "Mitch was so scary the first time I met him. Andie definitely softened him up."

He smiles at that. "What about you? Never been afraid of falling in love?" Colby lifts his glass to his lips and drains half of it in one gulp.

I can't help but notice the sturdy column of his neck, and the muscles that move when he drinks. "My goodness, you're like a camel."

"Now who's avoiding the serious questions?" he teases.

"Fine. No, I haven't. My parents are high school sweethearts. They made it look so easy. I thought I'd meet someone in college, get married, and have three kids before I even made tenure." I pause, taking a small sip of wine. "Then I met a guy in college. Fell head over heels. He was there on a hockey scholarship, and he was handsome. I was flattered he noticed me. But while I was planning our future together, he was screwing around with sorority girls."

Colby's face darkens and he mutters a nasty word to

himself. Colby doesn't look angry often, but when he does, it's intense. "What's his name?" He clears his throat, as if trying to dispel his own anger. "Does he play professionally?"

"Colby, it was a long time ago, no need to be angry. Last I heard, he was in the minor leagues, not sure which team or if he still plays. And his name is Travis."

His eyes narrow like he's deep in thought. "So, that's why you hate hockey players."

I grimace. "I don't hate hockey players."

"Yes, you do. You think we're all like that?" He seems genuinely annoyed, and I feel bad.

"I'll admit, I've been leery of athletes in general since the whole debacle. And some of the hockey players that come through my class are so cocky and lazy in their studies. Always expecting me to bend over backward for them, since some schools do. It gets annoying."

"I forget Arlington University has a D1 hockey program."

"Yeah." I bite my bottom lip, wanting to ask him a question, but nervous he'll agree with Dr. Hawthorne. "Do you think I should take it easy on them? Extend their deadlines?"

"Oh, hell no," he says seriously. "If they want to make it to the NHL, they need to get used to working their asses off. Coddling them is doing them a disservice."

A slow grin spreads across my face, and Colby stares at me with a confused expression.

"Stop that."

"Sorry, it's just that, for once, I agree with you."

His eyebrows raise and he smiles. "Oh, then continue with the creepy grin."

CHAPTER 15
COLBY

OUR FOOD COMES OUT, glazed duck for Noel, and filet mignon for me, and we eat in comfortable silence. Conversation flows easily between Noel and me, but the quiet pauses are nice too. I'm a guy who requires a lot of action, a lot of noise. But something about being in Noel's company calms my need to be in motion. That urge to always be moving—to always be *on*—is quelled, and I can simply sit and enjoy our time together. Maybe because I love looking at her so much. I could just sit here and look at her all day.

Remembering the fantasy convention happening tomorrow, I finish chewing my steak and swallow. "So, any other plans this weekend?"

She dabs at the corner of her mouth with her napkin. "Oh! Yes!" Her eyes light up with excitement.

I wonder if she'd be this free with Dr. Dickhead, and if she'd tell him all of her nerdy quirks. I bet he wouldn't love them as much as I do.

"My sister and my parents are coming to town tomorrow and we're going to a fantasy convention. We're dressing up as

Arwen and Galadriel from Lord of the Rings. We've been planning this for months."

"That sounds cool," I say, trying to keep my expression even, pretending I knew nothing about the fantasy convention. I pull a non-existent piece of lint from my sweater vest and flick it away, feigning ignorance. Her parents are coming as well. Now I can win them over too. Perfect.

A tall, lean, blond man approaches our table. His expression is relaxed and friendly.

Noel doesn't notice him at first, but when she does, her eyes go wide. "Dexter?"

She stands from her seat, and I mirror her action. The man leans in and does the European cheek-kissing thing, and I instantly want to punch him.

"Dr. Woodcock, funny running into you here," he says in a British accent. That's when I realize this is the guy. The professor who's too stupid to notice her. "This is my favorite restaurant. Do you come here frequently?"

"This is my first time, but it's lovely," she answers, smiling at him like he's the greatest thing ever.

I'm curious how he got a reservation here, seeing as I had to pull in three favors to get one. "I'm Colby," I say, thrusting my hand out in the Brit's direction.

Dexter grabs my hand with his lanky arm, athlete my ass, and shakes it. His grip is limp, and his handshake is weak. He just lost even more of my respect for this sad excuse of a handshake. "Yes, I know. Huge fan," he says.

"No kisses for me?" I tease, hoping my face isn't dark red with the unreasonable amount of anger bubbling up inside me.

He bursts into laughter. Noel quirks an eyebrow and offers an awkward chuckle as well.

"Sorry if I interrupted a date." Dexter's eyes move between me and Noel.

"Oh, no, Colby and I are just friends," she answers easily. Too easily.

Dexter looks quite pleased at this and takes his phone out of his back pocket. "Speaking of dates, I was hoping to ask you out soon, but didn't want to do it at work. Would you like to grab dinner soon? Or perhaps even a hockey game?" He winks at me.

Noel blushes. "Oh, yes. That would be great."

"Perfect. Give me your number and I'll add your contact information."

She spouts off her number while he saves it in his phone. My gut is telling me he's asking her out because she's here with me. Maybe because she seems more desirable when she's with another man, or perhaps he wants me to get him good seats at Eagles' games or something.

"Well, I'll leave you two to your evening," Dexter says. "And Noel, I will call you and set up a time for our date."

He excuses himself with a very British bow and we sit back down to finish our meal.

The moment Dexter is out of ear shot, Noel leans in. "Oh my gosh! Colby!" She bounces in her chair. "I can't believe that just happened. You're a miracle worker! Best dating coach ever."

"Ha. Right. Good thing we're doing these lessons." I force a smile, knowing she's excited and wanting to be happy for her. But it's hard to smile when I'm this irritated.

———

The following morning, my doorbell rings and I rush to the door, knowing my baby sister is on the other side. I realize three isn't necessarily a baby, but she'll always seem like a baby to me, I think.

Swinging the door open, my dad and Serenity come into view first. Dad is the mirror image of myself, just add twenty years or so. And Serenity looks like a vegan Barbie.

I feel Ruthie before I see her, her little body colliding with my legs as she wraps herself around me like a koala. "Cowby!" she says, not quite able to pronounce L yet.

Bending down, I lift her into my arms and kiss her chubby cheek before moving aside to allow my dad and his girlfriend room to step inside.

Dad gives me an awkward shoulder pat as he passes by me. "Good to see you, son."

I nod my head instead of saying anything. Because it's not good to see him, but as long as he brings Ruthie along, he can visit anytime.

"Oh, Colby! You're as handsome as ever," Serenity oozes once she's inside. "Not as handsome as your dad, but wow."

I smile and hope it doesn't look like a cringe. "Gee, thanks. Good to see you too, Serenity."

She chuckles and points to the hallway which leads to my master bedroom and the two lower-level guest rooms. They always stay in those rooms since there's no furniture upstairs yet. My dad rolls their suitcases down the hallway, and I wonder why they need two full-sized suitcases for only one night. My guess is that most of it is Serenity's stuff.

A sticky hand slaps against my cheek and I glance over at my sister. She's petting my face like I'm her own personal kitten. I burrow my face against her neck, rubbing my unshaven skin against her. She screeches and giggles. "Cowby! No!"

Serenity's voice pulls us from our fun. "Please don't make her hyper, Colby. I'm already getting a headache." She pulls Ruthie from my arms and settles her on her hip. Ruthie pouts for a second but calms down quickly enough, happy to be in her mother's arms. Serenity kisses the top of my sister's head, and they smile at each other.

For all the annoying things about my father's girlfriend, I can at least say she's a good mom. And for that reason alone, I'll be nice to her. But I *won't* pretend to like her cooking.

Dad comes back from dropping off the luggage to the guest rooms and folds his arms over his chest. "How's the preseason going? The rookies any good this year?"

"We have some good ones. There's a new defenseman too, thank goodness. Mitch could use more help. With the defensive strength, we might even stand a chance to win the cup this season."

He listens intently. "You came awfully close last season. I'd love to see you guys win it all."

The Eagles made it to the second-round last season. We were tied up with the St. Paul Grizzlies and then lost in overtime in game seven. If it hadn't been for that lucky shot, we would've made it to the final. Bruce is still reeling from the whole thing; I think he blames himself for not blocking that shot. But the issue was our defense, not Bruce's goal tending. Our defense has been weak for the last few years, and Mitch can't hold it together by himself.

"You and me both. If we strengthen our defense with some new blood, I think we could do it."

Dad smiles. He's a big sports guy. The only thing we have in common to talk about. "So, you have plans today?"

"I do, and I was hoping I could bring Ruthie along?" I direct my question at Serenity.

Ruthie squeals excitedly and we all laugh. "I think that's a yes," Serenity says.

"Oh, also… I know you're cooking tonight, Serenity, but I might be bringing some guests over for dinner. Thought I'd grill some burgers, so we have enough food." Because if I have it my way, Noel will be smitten by me and Ruthie's costumes and join us all for dinner, along with her family.

"No, no, no! You're already letting us stay here at the last minute. You're not lifting a finger tonight. I still have to run to the store for supplies, anyway. I'll just add burgers to my list." Serenity smiles at me sweetly.

"Wow, really? Thanks."

This day is coming together perfectly.

CHAPTER 16
NOEL

MY DAY HAS BEEN COMPLETELY DERAILED. If Mom and Dad wouldn't have changed all of our plans, me and Helen would've had enough time to get ready for the convention and head over there. Of course, my parents decided they wanted to visit Gram first, and then Gram wanted to come too. Now everyone is joining us at the convention, which is why I'm now surrounded by family members donning elf ears. Mom and Dad don't even have elfish clothes, it's just elf ears with jeans and sneakers. Gram at least wore a sparkly dress, so she's pulling off the elf look.

I don't mind hanging out with my parents, but they can be pretty dorky.

We walk inside the convention center; it's filled with people wearing cosplay and various booths where you can purchase books and cosplay accessories. There are a few authors signing books too, but the lines to see them are super long.

"Oh, girls! Look at these!" Mom says, clomping over to a booth in her white, New Balance tennis shoes. Dad joins her, wearing the same exact shoes but in a man-version. They might not look as bad if he weren't also wearing pleated jeans from the nineties.

Mom points to a shelf filled with handmade flower crowns. Some are dried flowers and others are silk. They're lovely and would look great with my Arwen inspired dress.

Helen rushes over and peruses the options. "They're gorgeous!"

Dad grins. "Alright, flower crowns for all my girls! On me."

"Thanks, Dad!" Helen gives him a peck on the cheek, then chooses a crown of baby's breath and tiny, pink roses.

I join them by the shelf and select one that is all white flowers, but has fake gemstones woven throughout. Mom surprises me and picks one out too. She usually keeps things pretty simple: tennis shoes, t-shirt, jeans. But she looks cute in the crown of purple flowers she chose.

Dad pulls out his big, clunky wallet and pays the man running the booth with a wad of cash.

"About time he uses some of that money he inherited," Gram's voice mutters from beside me. I snicker and she joins me. My parents are usually very frugal, and they certainly didn't get that from Gram.

"Oh, Mom, you pick one too!" Dad says when he turns and sees Gram is the only one not wearing a flower crown.

"Put your money away, I'll be fine," she tells him in a teasing voice, then links her arm through mine. Helen goes to Gram's other side and follows suit. The three of us walk in a row with Mom and Dad behind us.

Looking ahead into the crowd, a man dressed as Gandalf the Grey towers over the crowd. He's holding a small child, who's dressed as a hobbit, hairy feet and everything. His face is covered with a beard, and together they're the cutest thing I've ever seen. I allow my imagination to fly away for a second, and I picture coming to events like this someday with my husband and children, all dressed up together. How fun? I try to picture Dexter Hawthorne dressing in fantasy cosplay, but I can't quite see it. Something about him seems too prim and proper for all this.

To my surprise, Gandalf and Frodo walk straight toward me, stopping right in front of me, Gram, and Helen. It's the waggle of those dark, dark eyebrows that puts it all together for me. It's Colby. And this cute little Frodo has to be his sister because she is a teeny-tiny version of him.

Something I can only describe as butterflies, flurry deep in my stomach. Not only is this the cutest thing I've ever seen, but he came to this convention knowing I'd be here, *and* he's reading *The Hobbit*.

But why?

Sure, he's flirted incessantly with me over the past year, but that's just Colby. He flirts with Mel and Andie, too. It's his personality. But why would he make so much effort to like what I like, to show up where I am?

Because we're friends now? Yeah, that has to be it. He's helping me get Dexter's attention, after all. He wouldn't have agreed to be my dating coach if he was pursuing me for himself.

I huff a laugh. Even the idea of Colby Knight making such an effort to pursue *me* is ridiculous.

"Hello, young ladies. You all look lovely," Colby says, disguising his voice to sound like Gandalf. The child in his arms giggles, showing off her dimples. My goodness, she really is a tiny Colby, dimples and all. I'd never stopped to wonder what Colby looked like as a child, but he must've been beautiful, just like his sister. Goodness, what will his own children look like?

A strangled whimper leaves my parted mouth and Gram

looks at me with raised eyebrows. She has to recognize Colby's blue eyes and dark brows.

Helen, who's completely oblivious to the famous athlete standing before us, says, "Oh, my gosh! I love your costumes." She claps her hands together and Colby's sister does the same, making us all laugh. "You are the cutest little hobbit I've ever seen."

"Tanks!" Colby's sister says to Helen, then turns back to Colby. "I gotta go potty."

Those dark eyebrows go all the way up to is white wig. His eyes are so wide, it makes me wonder if he didn't think this through beforehand. Because he definitely didn't anticipate having to take the little hobbit to the men's restroom.

"Would it be okay if I took you? The ladies' restroom is much nicer than the boys'."

Helen's head snaps in my direction, probably wondering why I'd offer to take a random child to the restroom. Ruthie—I think is her name—looks to her big brother for confirmation that it's okay and he nods.

"Thanks, Noel. You're a lifesaver." Colby sets his sister on the ground, and she grabs onto my hand with one of her small ones and Colby's with the other. Together, the three of us walk toward the restrooms, and it feels strangely intimate. Like a glimpse of what it would be like to have a family. I shake the thought.

"So," I say. "What are you doing here?"

Colby gives me an abashed grin through his sleek, white beard. "Thought it would be fun to surprise you with our amazing costumes."

Ruthie reaches down and yanks the hair off one foot. "Yuck," she says, throwing it onto the carpet and leaving it behind. Colby simply shrugs and laughs.

"You were really just dying to dress up like a wizard?"

He levels me with a serious look, something out-of-character for this man. "Angel, maybe I just wanted to see you."

His steady gaze is making me feel rather hot under this floor-length dress and flower crown. His blue eyes drill into mine so deeply, I wonder if he can see right into my cerebrum. I feel as if he's desperate for me to understand the look he's giving me, that he wants to wordlessly convey something.

Ruthie tugs on my hand, and I glance down at her. Leaving the depths of one set of blue eyes, only to collide with another, smaller pair. Their resemblance really is uncanny.

The child tugs me into the bathroom, and I don't look back at her big brother in the process. Instead, I welcome the air that has filled my lungs once more now that I'm no longer looking at him.

I stand outside the bathroom stall while she does her business. When she comes out of the bathroom, she smiles at me, showing off those darling dimples again. I lift her so she can wash her hands and her eyes meet mine in the mirror. "You're pwetty."

I nearly blush. Children's compliments mean more than adults do because children are unfiltered and brutally honest. "Thank you. So are you. You look just like Colby."

She giggles so loud; it nearly bursts my eardrum. "You tink Cowby is pwetty."

Ruthie finishes washing her hands, and I set her down and hand her a few paper towels. "That's not what I meant," I say.

She rushes out of the bathroom, and I quickly trail behind her in case Colby moves from his spot outside the women's bathroom.

Ruthie stops right in front of her brother's feet and yells, "She tinks you're pwetty!"

Colby gives me a look that can only be described as cocky. And then he smirks. "Oh, really?"

I heave an exasperated sigh. "That's not what I meant!"

Gram, Helen, and my parents appear through a crowd of people, and I take a few steps in their direction, thankful for the interruption.

Colby is fast though, gently grabbing my elbow and leaning in to whisper, "don't be embarrassed. I think you're pretty too."

I swallow the lump that has formed in my throat and will the goosebumps that are now sprinkled across my skin, to go away. But the sensation of his whispered breath on my ear, won't go away so quickly.

"Oh, there you are!" Mom says. "We were wondering where you and the mysterious Gandalf disappeared to."

Colby steps in front of me, bowing slightly. "Ah, you must be Mrs. Woodcock?"

My mother, God bless her, blushes furiously. And she's not even getting the full impact since his face is covered with a beard. Proof that it's not all in a man's looks, it's in his confidence.

"Why, yes, I am!" She brings her hand to her chest. "And this is Mr. Woodcock." She places her other hand on my father's shoulder.

"Pleasure to meet you, I'm Gandalf. But also known as Colby Knight. And this is my little sister, Ruthie." She smiles up at my parents.

Helen gasps. "Colby Knight?! Like *the* Colby Knight?"

A few people around us turn and stare, Colby pulls his beard up in an effort to hide more of his face.

"Sorry," Helen whispers. "I'm Helen, by the way."

"And I'm Gram," Gram says with a saucy wink.

"Oh, I remember you. You naughty little minx." Colby shakes his head in dismay, but he's grinning.

These two are too much alike, I don't think it's a good idea for them to be in the same vicinity too long. I tug Gram away from Colby before the two of them can conspire anymore crazy plans. But the odds of her winning Colby in another auction are slim to none. I think...

"Oh, hey the line is finally shorter to see Susan Mawry! I want to get my book signed," Helen says, reaching into her canvas tote and pulling out Susan's debut romantic fantasy novel. I'm definitely borrowing that later.

"You kids go have fun," Dad says, slowing his steps. "Your mother and I are going to go get some food. Someone said they have turkey legs here." He looks very excited about the prospect.

"And baklava!" Mom shares in his excitement.

Gram leans in so only I can hear her, and whispers, "I'm going to go join the old fuddy duddies. You nail this one down while you still can." She jerks her thumb over her shoulder in Colby's direction.

"Gram," I whisper back. "We're just friends."

"You sure are a lot friendlier now than you were a few weeks ago." She gives me a knowing glance, then she hustles after my parents.

Now it's just me, Helen, Ruthie, and Colby, standing in the short line to see Susan Mawry. To my shock, Colby reaches into his robes and pulls out a copy of Susan's book.

Noticing my surprise, he explains, "I saw some authors would be here and wanted to be prepared. Plus, a werewolf and a fae princess? Yes, please."

"Right? Oh, my gosh. It was so good!" Helen raves, waving her hands around. "Did you love the part where he stayed in his wolf form for that steamy kiss?"

Colby's eyebrows raise. "I haven't started it yet, but now I'm even *more* excited to read it."

I snort a laugh. The vision of this large, muscular athlete

curled up on a sofa reading werewolf smut is too much.

"We could read it together," Colby says, his voice low and rumbly.

When my face breaks into a furious blush, he winks at me. The rascal.

It's our turn to see Susan, and she looks fantastic with her fake fangs and braided, black hair. She even went all out by dripping fake blood on her white dress and wearing red contact lenses.

"Oh goodness! That's the cutest little hobbit ever!" Susan says, her eyes going big and round as she takes in Ruthie's cuteness.

"Tanks!" Ruthie says, grabbing one of the lollipops on Susan's table, unwrapping it, and sticking it into her mouth before anyone can take it away from her. Something tells me big-brother-Colby wouldn't have taken it away, anyway.

Susan's eyes move to Colby and even with the red lenses, I see how they inspect him with an appreciative glance. Colby can hide his appearance with Gandalf robes, but he still oozes masculine charm and swagger.

"And hello, Gandalf." Susan winks, reaching her hand out in front of Colby like she's waiting for him to kiss it. Instead, he hands her a copy of her own book. "Would love it if you could make it out to Colby, your number 2 fan. I think Helen here is number 1." I can't see his face, but I can tell he's smiling by the sound of his voice.

Helen rushes forward. "I totally am! I absolutely loved The Werewolf and the Wings."

Susan smiles at Helen quickly then turns her attention on Colby again. "There are some hot scenes in this book. Did you enjoy them?" she purrs, finally taking the book from him, making sure to overlap their hands in the process.

The burning sensation coiling throughout my body is a

strange experience, and something I'm unfamiliar with. I feel oddly protective of Colby. He's just trying to get a book signed and she's treating him like a cone from the ice cream truck on a very hot day. Cool it, Susan.

Yes, it's the urge to protect that's running through my body. I'm almost positive. Even though I don't get sweaty when I feel protective over my siblings. And I've never been on the verge of slapping someone in their defense.

Colby, however, appears completely unaffected by the woman's obvious come-on. Which almost irritates me more. Should he be slapping her away? Gandalf would.

I remember our conversation at Pancake Palace about how all the female attention gets old. He's probably just being nice. For the first time, I see how suffocating all the attention must be. Here I am, on the opposite end of the spectrum, desperately trying to get Dexter's attention. But I hadn't stopped and wondered how it must feel to constantly be in the spotlight. It's something that would be fun at first but would get old really quickly. And as an introvert, that kind of attention would be my worst nightmare.

Susan signs Colby's book, keeping her eyes pinned on him the whole time. Then she kisses it, leaving a red lipstick mark right by where her name is now imprinted.

Helen clears her throat, a subtle reminder that she also has a book she wants signed. Susan finally looks at her. She smiles at my sister, but it's much less enthusiastic than the treatment she gave Colby. Suddenly, the urge to read her book disintegrates completely. Which is unfortunate, because one doesn't often get the opportunity to read a whimsical—but sexy—romance between a shifter and a fairy.

We spend another few hours walking around the convention. Helen doesn't seem upset by Susan's behavior, so I don't bring it up. Ruthie, who at first was delighted by the costumes and fun booths to look at, is growing bored with the whole thing.

"Cowby. I wanna go home." She pouts, reaching her arms upward so he'll pick her up.

He happily obliges, lifting her onto his shoulders. She smiles, happy for the time being. "I should probably get this one home; she's been on her hairy feet a lot today."

Me and Helen snicker, and I notice that there's only hair on one foot after she ripped the chunk off the other one earlier.

Colby shifts on his feet, appearing uncomfortable, maybe even awkward. "We're having a cookout tonight, burgers. It's just my dad, his girlfriend, Ruthie and myself. I thought you all might want to come over?"

"To your house?" Helen's voice comes out high-pitched and way too excited.

I jump in before she can say more. "Oh, no. We wouldn't want to impose on your family time."

"If it was an imposition, I wouldn't have invited you." He smirks like he's waiting for my next excuse.

I have nothing. I don't even know what I'm feeding my family tonight, or how everyone will fit inside my apartment. Colby's house is probably huge, and likely filled with food.

He studies me, most likely seeing the indecision playing across my face. He leans in, lowering his voice, and says, "Meeting the parents is something you need to learn. You know, for your lessons."

I'm glad he didn't say that loudly enough for my sister to hear, but she's studying us with interest. Those little sister eyes are alight with intuition, or so she thinks. Because there's nothing going on between me and Colby. But he's right, practicing meeting a man's parents *would* put my mind at ease for the future. "Let me check with Mom and Dad."

"And Gram," he says seriously. "Gram has to come too."

CHAPTER 17
COLBY

I CHECK my watch for the twelfth time in a two-minute time span, waiting for Noel and her family to arrive. I'm more nervous to show Noel my house and spend time with her parents than I've ever been before a big game.

On the drive back home after the fantasy convention, the thought popped into my head that Noel isn't the one who needs practice meeting the parents... I am. I've dated, philandered, whatever you want to call it. And I've unintentionally made a lot of women fall in love with me (or lust, perhaps) but I've never, ever, met the parents of a woman I had romantic feelings for.

I have no idea if parents like me, and I'm thinking they probably won't. My reputation isn't what parents want for their intelligent, wholesome daughters. They likely won't trust me. And my own father is here with his ridiculously young girlfriend, will they think that'll be me in twenty years?

None of this makes me look like marriage material. And for Dr. Noel Woodcock, I *want* to be marriage material. I want her parents to adore me. I want them to go home tonight and say,

"Noel, why don't you marry that wonderful young man? What a great guy!"

But they'll likely warn her away from me instead. Which probably explains why I'm pacing by my front door and my palms are damp.

Finally, I see two cars pull up, Noel's, and presumably, Gram's. Her family pours out of the vehicles, and I open my front door to greet them before they even knock, because I have zero chill with this girl.

Gram walks up the walkway ahead of the others, despite her son trying to hold her arm and help her. She tugs her arm away and gives him an annoyed stare.

I welcome Gram, Noel's parents, and Helen, holding the front door so they can come in. They all say sweet things about how gorgeous, and huge, my house is. But it's not their opinions and compliments I'm looking for.

Noel is the last one to trail through the front door. She's abnormally quiet, even wringing her hands together like she's nervous.

"Hey, angel. Thanks for coming." I give her a smile that I'm hoping will put her at ease and take away whatever nerves she might be experiencing.

She glances up at me with those golden-brown eyes, exhaling a shallow breath. "Thanks for inviting us to your bachelor pad."

"Ah, there she is with the snark. I knew she was in there somewhere behind this shy façade."

She laughs then lowers her voice. "Listen, Colby. My parents are dorky, I love them and I'm not ashamed of them. But they're not like your parents, trust me. They don't swear, they don't drink, they don't even watch movies that have language in them."

"Well, son of a biscuit. How will I ever behave myself?"

She rolls her eyes, but there's a smile there too. "I'm serious. I'm not sure why, but I don't want them to hate you. I guess you're my—"

I lean in, taunting her. "Your what? Come on, you can say it."

"Friend," she says with a groan.

Even though I hate that she's referring to me as a friend, I can still relish in the progress we've made. I'll take it, and I'll focus on that instead of the fact that she thinks her super-conservative parents won't like me.

Damn it. I mean, darn it.

"So, your parents have never even watched a Marvel movie?" I ask in a hushed whisper as I lead her inside.

"Nope. We grew up watching old BBC shows and historical documentaries."

"Wow. That explains why you're such a nerd."

She laughs and shoves me, just as we walk past the foyer where her family is waiting for us. Her parents look between us, their expressions half concerned, half amusement. Gram is beaming, looking thrilled to see her granddaughter giggling, and Helen grins at the sight. The same smile as her big sister's.

"Come into the kitchen and I'll introduce you to my dad and his girlfriend," I tell them, using an extended arm to show them the way. The entry is tall and grand. It's what sold me on the house, being the show-off I am—er, was. The flooring is white marble in a herringbone pattern and the chandelier that hangs above our heads is full of intricate crystals. My cleaning lady spends ten hours each month polishing them. I only know this since Ma is my cleaning lady, and she complains about it every month.

I lead them down the short hallway that leads from the foyer and into the spacious kitchen and dining room. Ruthie is running amuck, probably because I let her have sweets at the

convention. Dad is watching ESPN on his phone while flipping burgers on the grill in the outdoor kitchen, and Serenity is
at the stove, pulling out her infamous vegan casserole. Her
hair looks freshly blown out from her spa day, and if I'm not
mistaken… her hair is longer now. Must have gotten new
extensions.

"Oh!" Serenity says when she spots us. "Your guests are
here! Hi! I'm Serenity." She takes her apron off to reveal a very
tight, very revealing crop top. Mrs. Woodcock's eyes nearly fall
out of her head, and Mr. Woodcock looks down at his New
Balance tennis shoes.

"Nice to meet you," Gram says, not skipping a beat. "Love
your top, I need to get myself a few of those crop tops. They're
so trendy." She winks at Serenity, making her laugh.

Dad sees us through the double French doors that line the
wall between the outdoor kitchen and the dining room and steps
inside. It's easy to spot the external differences between my dad
and Noel's parents. My dad looks young, probably because his
skin is tan from laying out by the pool, and he works out a lot.
But also, he's vain. His appearance is important to him. He's
dressed in the latest trends, similar to the way a man in his midtwenties would dress. Sage green shorts that show off his quads,
and a simple grey tee that clings to his arms and chest. He hasn't
even started losing his hair yet. Maybe he never will. It's thick
and dark, just like it was in his wedding photos with my mother.

Noel's parents may not be stylish, but they put the effort in
to have a relationship with her. They didn't come to see her so
they could stay in her mansion and have a free babysitter, they
came to spend time with her. She says she's not embarrassed
by her parents. But I *am* embarrassed by my dad. Even though
he's cool by society's standards.

My dad doesn't care about me… he cares about status and

nice things. He cares about his looks, and showing off his hot, young baby mama.

Noel's parents get over the shock of Serenity's outfit quickly and move forward to shake her hand. Introductions are made all around.

My dad doesn't pay attention to his girlfriend, Ruthie, or my guests, he focuses completely on Noel. I'd be creeped out if he was checking her out, but he seems focused… like he's studying her. He keeps looking at me too, ping-ponging back and forth. Weird.

Ruthie recognizes Noel from earlier and comes to her side, grabbing her hand and smiling up at her. I wait to see how Noel reacts, and it's no surprise when she smiles down at my little sister and asks her how she enjoyed the convention. Speaking to her like she's a small adult, and not a baby.

"The casserole is ready!" Serenity announces, gesturing to the large pan on the stove top.

"The burgers are done too," Dad says, walking back outside and turns off the grill. He loads the burgers onto a large plate and comes back through the door, setting the plate on the counter for a buffet-style meal.

"Dig in," Dad announces, and everyone starts lining up for food.

I have a large dining room table, not because I have people over often, but because the house is so big it looked weird without one. There's plenty of room for us all at the table, and I'm glad it's useful for once. I sit between Gram and Noel and notice that Noel makes a weird face when she bites into her burger. She chews slowly, then swallows like she's eating sawdust. Inspecting my burger, I decide it looks normal enough and take a big bite. I stop mid-chew, wanting to spit the bite right back out. Serenity is watching all of us eat the dinner she and Dad prepared, her eyes are lit up like she's excited about it.

I force myself to swallow then wash the bite down with water. "Wow, Serenity. That's such an interesting flavor. What's in it?"

"Oh! I'm so glad you like it!" She claps her hands onto the table. "They're lentil burgers. Completely vegan, and you can't even tell!"

Noel makes a noise that sounds almost like a strangled sob, and I have to hold back a laugh as I say, "Yeah, it's, um, good."

"So, this meal is completely... meat free?" Gram asks, each word slow and calculated.

"Yes!" Serenity answers excitedly.

"Hmm," Gram muses.

Serenity grabs her bedazzled phone from the table and holds it up so Gram can see the background photo. The photo is of a chicken, a cow, and a sheep standing together, it's been photo-shopped to appear like they're smiling. "I always think to myself, if one of these little guys was here right now, would I be proud of what I was eating? And if not, what would I say to those cute faces?"

"I'd say, you look delicious," Gram mutters under her breath.

I choke on the bite of my lentil burger, full-on spluttering and pounding on my chest. Noel's hand comes to rest on my shoulder in a comforting gesture, like she wants to help but isn't sure how. The subtle pressure of her hand makes me forget I'm choking. The warmth of her skin through my shirt. I wish my shirt was off, so we could have skin to skin contact. Another time, Colby. Not when you're choking and keeping an old woman from offending your very dramatic, vegan, stepmom—or is it step girlfriend? Not sure what to label that.

After drinking my entire glass of water, my throat calms

down and I'm no longer fighting the urge to have another coughing attack.

Noel looks at me with concern, and I'd do just about anything to replicate this look on her again. Because she's looking at me like she wants to take care of me.

Oh, Angel, I would let you take care of me so good.

The doorbell rings and I pull up my phone to check who's there via the security camera. When I see its Remy, I tap the screen to talk and tell him to come on in. I stand and meet him as he's coming into the kitchen. He has a measuring cup in his hand and his eyebrows shoot up when he sees my table full of people. When his gaze lands on Noel, his lips turn up into a slow grin and he angles himself so only I can see his face.

"Nice," he says. "How'd you make that happen?"

"I'll explain later," I say through one side of my mouth, making sure no one can hear. "What do you need?"

"I need to borrow a cup of flour."

"And you think I have that?" I ask with a scoff.

Remy rolls his eyes. "Your mother cooks here every week, she has to have basic baking supplies stocked."

I shrug. "Help yourself."

He brushes past me and finds the baking supplies right away, scooping out a cup of flour and walking back toward the front door. He gives Noel a small wave, and she waves back. I don't miss the look of hero-worship on Helen's face. She's staring open-mouthed at my team captain like she has a shirtless poster of him in her bedroom back home.

I walk Remy to the door, and when we're alone, his calm demeanor completely changes.

"You went from trying to stop her from murdering you, to having family dinner? Dude! Those dimples are miracle workers." He chuckles at his own words.

"It's the BDE," I say, waggling my eyebrows.

"Gross." He wrinkles his nose and opens the front door to leave.

"I meant, big, dimple energy!" I yell after him as he escapes back to his own house next door. "Get your mind out of the gutter!"

After I get back to the table, we all force our vegan food down our throats. Under the table, I hold a napkin out to Noel so she can place what's left of her burger into it. She sneaks half her burger off her plate and onto the napkin with a whispered, *thank you*. Gram, the nosy scamp, clears her throat and raises one eyebrow. A silent plea for me to help her as well, which I do. She waits for Serenity to look away and sneaks her vegan casserole into the napkin.

When I get up to throw it away, my dad starts asking Noel questions from his seat across the table.

"So, Noel, what is it that you do?"

"I'm in my second year of teaching," she says proudly.

"Ah, elementary?" He steeples his fingers together on the table.

She chuckles. "No, I have a doctorate in history and teach at Arlington University."

His eyebrows shoot up. "Really? Wow. You know Colby never finished his degree, right?"

I take my seat again and level him with a confused stare. Because seriously, what the hell? "I was drafted by the NHL and couldn't finish, Dad. You act like I'm a moron. Plus, I only have a year left. I might go back and finish my bachelors someday."

"And what is it that *you* do?" Noel asks my father, her face totally serious. Her tone is almost defensive. I like it.

My dad puffs out his chest. "Actually, I'm a football coach."

I try not to laugh. My dad coaches peewee football at the high school where he's the custodian. I've never thought less of him for not having a college degree, and I didn't realize that was something he wanted me to have.

"In high school I was captain of the football team. Could've gone pro." He sighs, bringing his arms behind his head and stretching. "But football is so dangerous, you know? All the concussions and injuries."

"Right," Noel says, seeing right through the arrogant act. "Well, it seems you and Colby have both done pretty well for yourselves, despite not having college degrees." She makes a show of looking around my mansion.

I've never wanted to kiss her more. I've never wanted to kiss *anyone* more. Never in my life, can I remember someone standing up for me like this. Coming to my defense. My teammates are always there for me, on and off the ice, but it feels different having Noel here standing up to my dad.

"Of course." Dad chuckles awkwardly. "Didn't mean to make it sound like he wasn't successful." He clears his throat. "What do you do for fun?"

Another weird question, but Noel is rolling with the punches.

"Mostly I read, I love fantasy. Which is why we went to the fantasy convention earlier."

Dad's eyes flick to mine. "Wait, that's where you were at? With Ruthie?"

I lean back in my chair. "Yep! Noel is getting me hooked on phonics."

My dad looks befuddled, and honestly, mildly offended. I don't know why, what's wrong with a fantasy convention?

Ruthie scurries over to Dad's side and raises her arms, wanting him to lift her onto his lap. He peers at her with an annoyed expression, pulls a kid's show up on his phone, and hands it to her. "Not now, Ruthie, I'm busy. Here you go."

She looks disappointed for a split second before she starts watching the screen and sits on the floor beside his chair.

I glare at him, but he doesn't notice.

Noel's parents look slightly uncomfortable at the other end of the table as Serenity tells them her whole process in making the casserole. She's detailing the ingredients, as if they're going to make it for themselves someday.

Her dad has finally had enough and stands up. "Well, we better get Gram home. It's getting late."

Gram opens her mouth like she's going to tell him off, but with a look at Serenity, she nods her head. "Yes, please. I'm so, so tired in my old age."

Slowly, I swivel my head to stare directly at her, and she gives me a coy smile.

I'm bummed they're leaving, and that I have to spend the rest of the evening alone with Dad and Serenity. Maybe Ruthie will stay up and watch a movie with me. I realize this entire dinner was only tolerable because the Woodcocks were here, and it was really nice having them around. I'd rather spend time with Noel's parents, than with my dad.

Dad, Serenity and Ruthie say goodbye to our guests, and I walk Noel and her family to the front door. "I'm really glad you all came," I say, directing my comment to Noel.

Noel's dad shakes my hand with a firm handshake. "Loved getting to meet you, Colby. Hopefully we'll see you around again." He shoots Noel a look and she blushes.

"Likewise, Mr. Woodcock." I smile at him as he starts ushering the rest of the family outside.

Noel stays behind, looking at me intently, almost like she wants to stay. Or maybe she just feels bad for leaving me behind to deal with my dad and his vegan mistress.

"Thank you for having us, I'm relieved that someone is a worse cook than me," Noel says with a smirk.

I throw my head back in laughter.

Noel's mother must've heard her daughter's comment and whisper yells, "Noel! Manners!"

———

After Serenity and Ruthie are in bed that night, I attempt to stay up and watch some of the NHL preseason highlights on ESPN with my father. He, apparently, has other ideas and mutes the TV.

He turns to me, his forearms resting on his thighs as he sits on the sprawling sectional in front of my theater system. "Colby, what the hell is going on with you and this... professor?"

My eyebrows draw together. "What do you mean? She's a good friend of mine, and her best friend is married to Weston Kershaw."

"I know there's more going on than that. And I just don't get it." He shakes his head.

"Get what?" I ask, not bothering to correct him and tell him nothing is going on.

"You could have anyone you want. Hell, you could *do* anything you want. You're not tied down." He gestures toward the guest room where Ruthie is sleeping, and it makes me despise him even more. "You could have any woman you desire, in your bedroom right now. Actually, you could have three!" He huffs a laugh. "But you're... at fantasy conventions with a nerdy, academic type?"

I take a breath, collecting myself before I speak. "I guess that's the difference between you and me, Dad."

"What?" His face reddens.

"I may have thought that was the best life. But I grew up and grew out of it before I turned thirty. I wish I would've grown out of it sooner, or never even entered it. What a waste of time, pursuing women I wouldn't want a life with. Wouldn't want a family with." I pause. "But Noel? I'd be honored. Lucky. To have someone as caring, intelligent, and amazing as her by my side. Fantasy conventions and all."

Dad stares at me with his mouth partly open, as if he has no words. No retort for what I just leveled him with.

I stand and leave the room before I say anything I might regret.

CHAPTER 18
NOEL

THE MORNING after dinner at Colby's place, I'm having brunch with my family at a local restaurant before they head back to Maryland. Being around Colby's dad last night makes me incredibly grateful for my own. I hate that his dad is such a jerk. I never even saw that man pay attention to Ruthie once, or his girlfriend for that matter. He was too busy asking me prying questions, and judging Colby. And why? Colby is extremely successful.

I'm taking a sip of coffee when my mother places her hand on top of the one I'm not using. I set my mug down and look at her. Her eyes are filled with affection, she quickly glances at my dad, who's seated on my other side.

Helen is across from me, happily eating a muffin, and oblivious to the way Mom and Dad are smiling at me.

"Sweetheart, are you and Mr. Knight seeing each other?" Mom asks.

Dad hums and nods his head. "You two would make a cute couple."

Mom claps her hands together. "Oh, and he and Ruthie were absolutely darling at the convention!"

"He was so different from what I would've expected with his reputation and all." Dad chuckles. "But he's a genuinely nice guy. We really enjoyed him."

Helen drops her muffin, listening intently. She's been staying with me, but our parents have stayed at Gram's place. So, she obviously missed whatever conversation Mom and Dad had last night after dinner.

"Mom, Dad, you're right, he *is* great. But nothing is going on between me and Colby."

One of Mom's eyebrows arches. "I know we're not hip and cool anymore, but we're not blind."

"Whether you realize it or not, there's definitely something going on between you and Mr. Knight," Dad says with a knowing look.

Helen grins. "Oh yeah. The way you two stare at each other…" she sighs and falls back in her seat, fanning her face dramatically.

"I don't think we're right for each other," I argue.

"Do you feel that way because of his past? Because people can change," Dad says. "This may surprise you, but I was quite the ladies' man myself back in the day."

"Oh, yes. I practically had to fight the girls off with a stick!" Mom smiles fondly at him.

My brothers are quite handsome, so I don't have a hard time believing it. But I have to withhold a giggle since my dad is now sitting here with glasses and pleated, denim shorts.

"Colby is just a flirt. You guys are reading into this way too much. We're just friends."

Dad puts his hands up in defeat. "Okay, whatever you say."

"Plus, there's this really nice professor at work, and I'm hoping we have a date soon." I smile, still trying to convince them all that I'm not interested in Colby. "He asked for my phone number a few days ago."

I should be thrilled that Dexter finally asked for my number. But for some reason, I'm not as excited about the prospect of a date with him as I thought I would be.

"Oh sweetie! That's great." Mom rubs my shoulder affectionately.

Helen perks up again. "Oooh, the British one? You have all these hot guys fighting over you," she groans. "I want to move to the city and meet hot guys."

"You're way too young to be worrying about that," Dad says sternly.

I stifle a laugh and share a secret look with my sister. A look that says, *'our parents are ridiculous.'*

———

Monday morning, my lecture ends, and the students file out of my classroom. The hockey boys, of course, stop to talk to me. They both appear to be annoyed, and entitled, as usual.

"Hey Dr. Woodcock," the blond one says, swooshing his hair out of his eyes. "Listen, our game went into overtime last night and we weren't able to study for this morning's quiz. So, we're going to ask one more time for an extension before we give you a bad rating on Rate Your Professor Dot Com."

Wow. Shaking in my boots. "I'm sorry you guys are having a hard time keeping up with your studies. And I understand your hockey schedule is grueling. But what if you make it to the NHL? You'd be balancing brand deals, team activities and duties, and possibly even a family someday. You'll be working hard. You'll have a lot to juggle. Maybe this is preparing you for that." I give the boys my kindest smile. "And that's coming straight from the mouth of my good friend, Colby Knight."

Their faces go from annoyed, to amused. A second later, they're both cracking up. "Wow, good one Dr. W." The dark-haired one can barely talk in between bouts of laughter.

"Yeah, she's great friends with Colby Knight," the blond one titters. "That's the funniest thing I've heard all year.

Their jabs don't bother me. In fifteen years, they'll be like Colby's dad, talking to people about how they could've gone pro. And I'll be tenured by then. Probably married to Dexter with a couple of ridiculously smart children. Only, it's not Dr. Hawthorne I'm picturing. Instead, I'm picturing a man with dark hair and rippling arm muscles, rolling around on the floor wrestling with children. Children who have the same dark hair and bright-blue eyes as their handsome daddy. *Daddy Colby.* I break into goosebumps and have to close my eyes for a moment and force myself to replace the daydream with Dexter instead. I've obviously been spending too much time around Colby, that's all this is. I'm definitely not drawn to him in an effervescent way that I can't explain.

"Believe what you want, but I cannot offer you an extension or a makeup test without it being unfair to the rest of my students."

Their laughter ends abruptly, and they scowl at me as they leave my classroom, muttering under their breath that they should've taken Dr. Hawthorne's class. The dean told me last week they applied for a transfer, and when she saw their reason why, she denied the request.

I grab my phone to see if I have any missed messages and rest my back against my desk.

I have two missed texts, one from an unknown number. I open that one first.

UNKNOWN

> Dr. Woodcock, might I call you Noel? This is Dr. Hawthorne. You may call me Dexter. I was hoping to catch you at the coffee shop this morning, but you weren't there.

I smile at his formality. I can hear his British accent in my head telling me I *may* call him Dexter.

NOEL

> Good morning, Dexter. Yes, you may call me Noel. :-)

I save his number on my phone.

DR. DEX

> I would still love to grab dinner soon. What evening works for you?

NOEL

> I'm free this weekend!

Oops, I cringe. Maybe that was too desperate.

DR. DEX

> Would Friday work? I got tickets to the Eagles' game that night too. We could grab an early dinner, then check out the game?

I bite my bottom lip, feeling conflicted. A hockey game would be the last thing I'd normally want to do on a date. But I've never been to a game, despite begging from Andie and Mel. And there's a part of me that wants to see what it's all about, and to see Colby in serious-work-mode. Or does he grin and goof off the whole time? I'm curious because he's my friend. My pal. Andie's little brother, Noah, is also my friend. I've gone to his youth hockey games, so what's the difference?

Also, the noise of the arena would take away my need to fill awkward silences.

Friday works, and that sounds fun!

Dexter asks for my address and tells me he'll pick me up at five. He also reminds me to dress warm for the game, which feels so obvious it's almost condescending.

"He's just being nice, Noel. Sheesh. Give the guy a break," I mumble to myself as I pull up my other missed message. This one is from Colby and an easy smile tugs at my lips. I try to keep my expression neutral, because I shouldn't be smiling bigger over my text from Colby than my text from Dexter. I've wanted Dexter to ask me out, or to even notice me, since he started teaching here. And Colby hasn't even been on my radar. I've purposely ignored the man, even found him to be obnoxious. So, what's this annoying, new, sparkly feeling all about?

COLBY

Finished The Hobbit. SO EPIC. Starting The Fellowship of the Ring today.

NOEL

That's amazing! I'm impressed. Not everyone appreciates the slower pace of Tolkien's storytelling.

COLBY

How's your day going?

NOEL

Good! Actually, Dexter asked me on a date. We're going to dinner Friday... and an Eagles' game.

It takes Colby a full minute to respond, with the three dots appearing and disappearing over and over again.

COLBY

That's great! And if the date is boring, at least you'll have a bunch of hot hockey players to distract you.

I roll my eyes, but I'm grinning. I can always count on Colby to make me laugh.

NOEL

Oh, hey. Funny story. The hockey guys in my class didn't believe you're a friend of mine.

COLBY

Oh, is that right?

CHAPTER 19
COLBY

"SHE'S GOING on a date with him!" I run my hands through my hair, probably ripping half of it out of my head, as I stomp into Remy's gym. Remy, Bruce, West, and Mitch are staring at me, everyone appears concerned but Mitch. He looks annoyed, and like he'd rather be making out with Andie than working out with us during his off time before the season officially starts.

We had an early practice this morning and can easily fit in another workout. Plus, I need to work out some aggression after spending the weekend with my dad. And this is one of our last chances to work out together at Remy's. Our training schedule during the season is intense, not to mention traveling about every other week. And promotional stuff for the team.

"I mean, wasn't that a given?" Mitch asks. "You've been her dating coach this whole time. Which, I realize was a ploy to spend time with her. But she's gotta go on at least one date with this pickleball schmuck to realize he's not the one for her, right?"

Bruce nods enthusiastically. "Yeah! That's true."

"You have to kiss a few toads to find a prince, right?" West asks with a half-smile, half grimace.

I rest my fists on my hips. "Ideally, she'd only be kissing me."

Remy grabs the dry erase marker off the ground and walks over to our list, which surprisingly, he never erased. He taps the end of the marker on our list. Right where it says I need to kiss Noel.

"Desperate times, call for desperate measures. Time to kiss the girl," he says seriously.

"But he hasn't won over her family yet!" West argues, pointing to the list.

Remy shakes his head. "He had her family over for dinner a few nights ago. This changes everything."

Bruce gasps. "You what?"

"It's not a big deal. I invited them over after the fantasy convention." I shrug, taking a seat on one of the weight benches.

West emits a low whistle. "Dude. That for sure speeds the process up. Now you can move on to the kiss."

I glance around the room at my friends and teammates, they all have a matching look of determination on their faces. "So, time to kiss her?" I'm definitely not mad about this change of pace.

"Agreed," Mitch says.

"Anything else you can do to raise the stakes?" West asks.

"Actually, and I might need Mel's assistance with this, but there are two hockey scholarship punks in her class. They're always trying to get out of work... *and* they didn't believe that she knows me."

"You're kidding," Remy says, crossing his arms. "What if they go pro? Do they not realize how hard they'll have to work?"

"That's exactly what I said. And what better way to get the point across, than to tell them in person." I lift my eyebrows once.

The boys grin.

"I'm sure Mel will be more than happy to help," West says with a shit-eating grin.

"Time for me to go back to class and help out a certain professor."

———

When I walk back over to my house after working out with the guys, I hear Italian music blaring through my speakers. Ma is in the dining room, sweeping while she sings and dances along to the music. I can smell something amazing cooking in the oven, and there are remnants of flour covering my large, marble countertop. Probably from making homemade pasta or bread. It's the kind of smell that makes your mouth water, a scent that makes a house feel like a home. Vastly different from the scent of Serenity baking that horrible casserole. I'm not against vegan food, I've had some great vegan food. But never when it's been cooked by Serenity.

"Hey, Ma!" I announce myself as I enter the room, so I don't scare her.

She startles anyway, turning to glare at me with the broom in her hand. Her shoulders relax when she sees me, and she smiles adoringly. The endearing smile of a mother who loves her baby boy, even though he's thirty. She's wearing old jeans and sneakers with a plain white tee and a D.C. Eagles apron that I gave her as a joke on Christmas, but she loves it.

"There's my boy," she says, pulling the remote for my surround sound system out of her apron pocket and turning down the music. "How's training? I've barely seen you lately."

I lean against the wall as she moves into the kitchen to check on whatever she has in the oven. "I know, things have been busy. And Dad and Serenity came this weekend." I try to keep my face neutral, not letting her know Dad was a huge asshole, not that she'd be surprised. But Ma is happy now, she's doing great. I don't want to pull her into Dad-drama.

She puts oven mitts on, opens the oven, turns the pan, then closes the oven door. "How's that sweet little Ruthie?"

"Adorable as always. And nothing but trouble," I say with a grin.

"Sounds just like her big brother," Ma teases. "And my goodness, she looks just like you too!" She points to the picture of Ruthie hanging on the stainless-steel fridge with an oven mitt. "The kitchen and dining room were a mess. Did you have a party? I thought you were past that."

"Actually, Dad and Serenity were making a big meal, and I invited Noel and her family over for dinner. They had to endure Serenity's vegan cooking." I chuckle.

My mother's face instantly falls, but she forces a smile, trying to cover it.

"What's wrong?" I ask, confused. Ma has never been upset by me spending time with Dad. And she couldn't care less about his girlfriends anymore.

"Noel's the girl you like?" she asks carefully.

"She is. She's the *one*, Ma. She just doesn't know it yet." Suddenly, I feel embarrassed and stare down at my feet. My one-sided infatuation must sound ridiculous. I'm definitely leaving out the part about her going on a date with another man this weekend.

"And you introduced her to your dad, but not to me and Charlie?"

Ahh, now I understand. "No, it's not like that. Inviting her over was an easy excuse to spend time with her, and to get to know her family. When I introduce her to you, it will be because she knows that I love her. It will be when she loves me too. It will be when we're ready to move forward together. Introducing the two most important people in my life to each other is a big deal. But I *will* introduce you two, someday."

Ma clutches her chest. "Oh Colby. You're such a sweetheart. How could she resist you?"

I blow out a slow breath. "Well, I have a certain reputation. One that doesn't scream *future husband*."

She nods in understanding. "You have to earn her trust."

"I do. And I'm trying."

CHAPTER 20
NOEL

IT'S THURSDAY, the evening before my date with Dexter. I'm at Gram's house for dinner, we ordered food from our favorite French bistro a few blocks from her place. But I'm distracted, I have countless thoughts and feelings swirling around inside of me, my senses are overwhelmed. My chicken barely has any taste to it. It's like my brain is so overwhelmed it can't make my taste buds work properly.

"Okay," Gram says, dropping her fork onto her beautifully set table. She even has fresh flowers and a few candles lit. Gram knows how to throw a dinner party, even when it's only me.

"What's going on in that mind of yours? You usually eat that chicken in about five minutes flat."

"I do not! I'm not an animal." I put my own utensils down and sit back in my chair.

She quirks an eyebrow. "Whatever you say."

Gram is doing that thing where she's staring me down so intently, I wonder if she can read my thoughts. With a sigh, I tell her everything that's going on. She's a great listener, and

I've always confided in her. I should've told her about Colby being my dating coach sooner, but it sounded so stupid.

"And now I finally have a date with Dr. Hawthorne, but I'm not as excited as I should be. I've spent so much time with Colby lately, that my heart does this weird thing when he texts me, but it doesn't when Dexter texts me. And I'm so nervous about this date that sometimes I can't breathe! Oh, and I'm pretty sure I'm a terrible kisser!"

"Alright, sweetheart, let's take a deep breath."

I listen, closing my eyes and breathing deeply. I already feel better.

"So, you've essentially been dating Colby, and calling it lessons?" She asks slowly.

"No! Not at all. We just set up scenarios similar to if I was dating someone, so I can have practice. Then when the real thing happens, my awkwardness won't take over." As I say it, I realize she's correct. I've practically been dating Colby Knight. How could I be so stupid? Of course, I'm confused. For weeks I've been spending all of my free time with a sexy hockey player, convincing myself this was all for future dates with someone else.

Gram smirks knowingly. "Colby is a very handsome and charming man; I can see why you'd be confused. Not to mention, he obviously has feelings for you."

I scoff. "No. He doesn't. He *thinks* he does. I'm the only woman who didn't rip my clothes off for him the moment he made eye contact. I'm a novelty, a challenge."

"You know, you're pretty dumb for a smart person."

"Gram!"

She chuckles. "That boy looks at you like you hung the moon. I noticed it the night of the gala, and again at the fantasy convention." She pats my hand. "If Colby only wanted to sleep with you, he wouldn't take the time to attend nerdy conventions to impress you. He wouldn't invite your family over for dinner. He wouldn't give you *dating lessons*." She rolls her eyes. "He doesn't act like he wants one night with you. He acts like he wants *all* the nights with you."

I'm processing her words as she says them, and they actually make sense. But why would Colby want me? An uptight book nerd who spends her evenings at home. A girl no one ever notices.

"And what would make you think you're a bad kisser?"

Her question pulls me from my thoughts. I'm not sure Gram ever found out about my college boyfriend. I wasn't even worried about my brothers ruining his life after he broke my heart, but Gram? She would've hired a hitman or something. She tends to be unhinged.

"I had a boyfriend my junior year of college. His name was Travis," I explain. "Me being young and naïve, I thought I'd meet someone in college and get married after graduation. Just like Mom and Dad." I smile and Gram smiles back at me. Her eyes are soft, like she can already tell where this story is going. "He was handsome and charming, like Colby, and he was on a hockey scholarship. He was my first kiss, my first *I love you*." I sigh, hating that I gave him those things. "I genuinely thought Travis loved me. He did all the right things, said all the right things. We were together for almost a year. Then he was tagged in a video that went viral across campus. It was of him in a hot tub with three girls, there was very little clothing involved."

Gram's face is calm, but I can tell she's getting angry. It's in the way she's breathing short, shallow breaths. She's trying to remain in control, but really, she wants to find this guy and make him wish he'd never been born. It reminds me of Colby's reaction when he found out someone had cheated on me. Travis better hope Gram and Colby never gang up on him.

"Anyway, when I confronted him, he told me he was getting bored with me. Oh, and that I was a terrible kisser." I sigh. "So, he left our relationship with a bunch of new girlfriends, and I left it with a shell of the self-confidence I'd had beforehand."

"Does Colby know about this?" Gram asks, surprising me with her question.

I huff a humorless laugh. "Yeah. He looked as murderous as you do now."

"Good." Her jaw is clenched, but she takes a sip of her drink, trying to calm down. With a deep breath, she asks, "and this is why you're fighting your feelings for Colby? You think he'll be the same as this Travis guy?"

Biting my bottom lip, I consider her question before answering. "Honestly, yes. Colby feels dangerous. Looking at him makes my world tip on its axis. Thinking about him makes my stomach feel strange. I think he's capable of hurting me in ways no one else ever could. He has a power over me that I don't like."

She smiles knowingly, maybe that's how she felt about my grandfather too. "I understand. And you think the professor is safe? You think you could have feelings for him too?"

"Yeah, I think we make sense. I find him attractive, and I've wanted him to ask me out for a while. Shouldn't I at least go on the date?"

Gram takes a moment to think. Her barely visible grey eyebrows drawing together. "Go on your date with the professor. You already said yes. But when you're out with him, really try to see if you can picture a future with him. And if you could have chemistry."

I nod and open my mouth to speak, but she brings her hand up gesturing for me to shut up.

"I'm not finished. Go on this date with the professor, but

don't kiss him. Kissing one man when you're thinking of another would make you no better than that sleazy college boyfriend of yours."

"Fair enough."

"And sweetheart," Gram says, leveling me with a serious stare. "Someone is only a bad kisser if they have the wrong partner. And something tells me Colby could teach you plenty about kissing. Maybe take advantage of those dating lessons." She gives me a saucy wink.

CHAPTER 21
NOEL

FRIDAY NIGHT, Dexter picks me up from my apartment and drives us to a UK style pub downtown near the arena. After the drive here, where the conversation lagged, I'm thankful for the noise of the pub. We're seated in comfortable leather chairs at the bar. Dexter ordered an IPA and I got some fancy, fruity cocktail called *The Eagle*. The bar, floor, and walls are all polished wood, but it gives the place a cozy vibe. A pregame sports show is playing on screens all around the pub and the place is buzzing with excitement about the game.

I know Mel and Andie are already there, probably taking cute photos in their matching jackets that have West and Mitch's numbers on the back. They've already grouched at me for going to a game tonight with Dexter, when I've refused their invitations for the past year.

I didn't think I could ever stomach hockey again, and all the memories it would drag up. But Colby seems to have replaced my memories of being cheated on with his big smile, and even bigger dimples. I brush the thought of the dimpled hockey player out of my mind. I promised myself I'd focus 100 percent on Dexter tonight. I owe it to him, and to myself, to give this a chance. To see if we could hit it off.

But even the drive here made me wish for the easy conversation and companionable silence I have with Colby. Or his flirtatious, teasing comments that keep me from having to fill the silent spaces. It's like Colby takes up every space, silent or loud. Big, or small. He pours himself in and fills every crack. Maybe that's what he did to my heart.

I sigh heavily as it occurs to me that I'm thinking about Colby, again.

Dexter is watching the pregame interviews intently, but turns to look at me suddenly. "The two boys in your class were denied their request to switch to mine. How are things going with them. Are they passing?"

"They're doing alright. Passing, but barely." I force a smile. "I told them about the study group that meets in the library, and they didn't act interested. Of course, I want all of my students to succeed, but their hockey schedule and training regime, has not changed from what they expected before starting at Arlington University. I still don't feel like I should I extend their deadlines."

He nods, listening with interest. "Right. You have a point. But the hockey program does bring in a lot of money for the school."

I smile back at him, scrunching my face up in a *that's cute* expression. "So, did you ask me on a date to talk about work? Or?"

He huffs a laugh and shakes his head. "No, of course not. Sorry, I can be laser focused on work sometimes."

I give him a genuine smile this time, allowing myself to relax. "Yeah, we have that in common. If I'm not thinking about work, I'm doing research on something or other."

He chuckles. One of the bartenders comes over to take our

order. We both request the fish and chips. When the bartender leaves us, Dexter turns to me again. His dark eyes gaze into mine, they're different than Colby's bright blues, but very pretty. His strong jaw is also attractive. Tonight, he's more casual than usual, in dark jeans and a Remington jersey for the game. "What do you like to do when you're not working or researching?" he asks.

"Read. I love to read," I answer quickly.

His face brightens and I feel hopeful for the first time since he picked me up. Finally, we have something in common besides work. "What do you enjoy reading?"

"I adore fantasy. Lord of the Rings is a favorite. But I also love anything with romance. The classics, like Jane Austen and the Brontë sisters, or even contemporary novels."

He wrinkles his nose. "Romance, really? I'm surprised you're into all of that fluff."

"Romance isn't just fluff. Romance gives people joy and hope in the form of a beautiful story. What could be better than that?"

"Karl Marx, Socrates, Aristotle."

I groan. "You enjoy sports but have the most boring TBR ever."

"I'm sorry, what's a TBR?" He looks offended.

Wow, this is going great. "To be read. A list of books you're going to read."

His face softens, and he laughs. "Those philosophers aren't on my," he gives a haughty pause. "T. B. R. I've already read them all."

I want to slow-clap for him and tell him he's a good boy, but I hold back. We still have an entire hockey game to get through. "You don't even like J. R. R. Tolkien?"

He lifts one shoulder in a shrug. As if J. R. R. Tolkien isn't even worthy of a double-shouldered shrug. "*The Lord of the*

Rings is alright, I guess. I actually thought the movies were better."

My jaw drops, but he doesn't see it because our food arrives. Thank goodness, something to keep our mouths busy so we don't have to make conversation anymore. Why did I think we'd be a good match? Besides the fact that we both have a doctorate in history, we have absolutely nothing in common. Maybe Gram was right, maybe I do need more spice.

CHAPTER 22
COLBY

I'M WOUND UP, shoulders tense, head throbbing. I wonder if this is how Mitch used to feel before games, before he went to therapy and got engaged to the girl of his dreams. If this is how he felt, it's no wonder he wanted to punch everything.

West is standing next to me in the tunnel we enter the ice from. The starting lineup is about to be announced before the game starts. He jabs me with his elbow. "What's wrong with you tonight?"

Bruce hums thoughtfully. I can barely see him since he's strapped into his full goalie gear. "Yeah, I was wondering the same thing. You're giving pre-Andie Mitch vibes."

"Hey," Mitch says from across the hallway, crossing his arms and bristling like he's offended.

I take my helmet off and hold it against my side. "She's here tonight. Noel is finally at one of our games, but she's on her date with *that guy*."

"Dr. Dickhead?" Remy asks from the back of the line, since the team captain is last to be announced, being the most antici-pated player.

"The one and only," I say.

West's mouth pulls up in a slow, mischievous grin. "You know, you could have some fun with the jumbotron. Do you know where they're sitting?"

"Not a clue."

"We'll all be on the lookout," Bruce says right before we hear his name announced. He turns and skates onto the ice, waving to fans as they cheer him on.

"We need a code for when we spot her, then we can alert you," West says, looking too excited about the whole thing.

Mitch grunts. "How about, hey Colby, there's Noel." We hear Mitch's name announced from the speakers and he skates out next. He gives one subtle wave to the crowd, and they go wild for it.

"That's too boring," West says, looking down as he thinks. "Oh, I know! We'll wave our arms like an eagle's wings and caw."

Remy shakes his head. "Speak for yourself, assistant captain. There's no way in hell I'm caw-ing like an eagle."

West tsks. "Terrible sport for a team captain."

My name is called before I can respond to his insane eagle idea. But I'm looking forward to him making an ass of himself, and hope he spots Noel first so I can see it in action. When I move onto the ice, I make a full circle, waving at fans and winking at the camera. I used to love that most of the cheering during my grand entrance sounded female. Lots of whistling and waving of big signs. And tonight is no different, but it doesn't give me the same thrill it used to. I look around the full arena, hoping to spot Noel, but it's impossible with all the signs. One of them says, *Colby, you can be my daddy toKnight!*

Points for creativity. But if it's not Noel holding the sign, I don't care. I skate toward center ice with the rest of my teammates as West and then Remy get their moment in the spotlight.

Once everyone is on the ice, a vocalist comes out and sings the national anthems, USA and Canada, then we get into place for puck drop. Meaning, there's no more time to search for Noel and her date. And that's the last thing I should be focused on right now. The first game of the season is a big deal. It can set a mood for the rest of the season. And we want to start off strong, especially with the new defensemen the Eagles signed after training camp. He's a rookie, but we all have high hopes. And there's the guy from the minor leagues too, but he's still out of commission from pulling a muscle.

The captain of the Pittsburgh Phantom's snatches the puck during the faceoff, but Remy is fast, faster than the other guy is expecting. He snags the puck back, taking it into the offensive zone. The Phantom's players are waiting for him though, blocking him from getting too close to their net. He zooms forward but sends the puck backward through his legs in a move we've practiced many times. I catch it and skate around his right side where they're not expecting me, aim and then shoot it straight above the goaltender's head. The crowd is screaming and going wild. Man, I've missed this. The roar of the crowd, the thrill of playing. I think it's even more exciting knowing Noel is here somewhere.

Unfortunately, the Phantom's goalie snatches the puck, just barely, in his glove.

Damn. Scoring in the first minute would've been a great way to get the game started, and it might've impressed Noel. Actually, knowing Noel, she's probably reading a book right now and not even paying attention. The thought makes me smile to myself.

I remember she's here with another man and that wipes the

smile off my face real fast. Is he holding her hand? Will he kiss her at the end of the date? And what if she kisses him back?

We get into position for the faceoff. Remy is staring down the Phantom's captain across from him. Remy steals the puck, determined to try to score a goal while we're still on the offensive end of the ice. The Phantom's captain lunges forward with his stick, trying to sweep it out from Remy, but Remy shoots it to West. West skates behind the net with the puck, a Phantom defenseman on his trail. When he arrives back in front of the net, he acts like he's going to shoot the puck, but sweeps it back over to Remy instead. Remy nails the puck with the perfect slapshot, and it flies into the top corner of the net before the goalie can stop it. The buzzer goes off and the fans filling the arena go so wild, you can barely hear the buzzer. We all skate over and embrace our captain, celebrating the first goal of the game, and of the season.

I'm on my way back to the bench to switch out for a water break, when I hear a loud, "Caw! Caw!" I peer over my shoulder, and West is, idiotically, flapping his arms like an eagle, then using his stick to point into the stands. My eyes immediately swing to Noel and the professor. A grin takes over my whole face, I can't help it. She's lovely, wearing a simple white sweater in a sea of red jerseys. She always sticks out in a crowd, my angel.

I'm surprised I didn't notice her sooner. She and Dr. Hawthorne are seated about four rows back from the glass, right behind our net. I stare at her for a full minute, hoping she'll look at me. But she and her date are having a conversation. His attention flits between her face and the game. I'm not sure I could split my attention with this girl and anything else. If she was seated beside me, and we were on a real date. Noel would have *all* of my focus.

Two women in front of Noel notice my stare and think it's

them I'm looking at. They stand and point to their red t-shirts that they've painted and decorated. One has dark hair, and her shirt says, *Future Mrs. Knight.* The redhead beside her has a similar shirt, but hers says, *right wing is my favorite position.* That makes zero sense, but whatever.

Noel glares at the backs of their heads and then rolls her eyes. I feel my lips tugging upward again, and Noel finally glances over at me. I wink at her dramatically, and she shakes her head slowly from side to side. But she's smirking.

The women in front of her think my wink was for them, and they're jumping up and down screaming. Noel ignores them, focusing solely on me.

CHAPTER 23
NOEL

ONE MINUTE left in the third period, and the Eagles are tied with the Phantom 3-3. I have to admit, I've enjoyed the game more than I expected. Probably due to a certain blue-eyed, dark-haired man who has the attention of every girl in this arena. But I'm still hoping they don't go into overtime. Because that will only prolong this date.

If I have to listen to one more comparison between hockey and pickleball, I will literally throw this Coca-Cola in Dexter's face. Okay, not really. But I might fall asleep.

Dexter's commentary isn't the only thing bugging me, but also the fan girls in front of us. I've heard Mel and Andie talk about puck bunnies, and I vaguely remembered the obsessive female fans from attending Travis's college games. But wow, female NHL fans are a whole different breed. The sheer number of signs and t-shirts shouting out Colby Knight is ridiculous. All the guys have signs made for them, but I can't help but notice that all of Colby's fans appear to be women. This shouldn't bother me, and I don't want it to. Not only do I have no right to feel possessive and jealous over Colby, but I don't want to judge him for his past.

"So," Dexter's voice interrupts my thoughts. "Do you think you could introduce me to the team sometime? That would be incredible."

I swing my head over to look at him, not knowing what to say. I don't plan on going on anymore dates with him, therefor, I'll never have the opportunity to introduce him to the team. "Yeah, maybe," I say with a shrug.

He seems happy enough with that answer and turns his focus back on the game. His eyes widen and he moves to the edge of his seat, which tells me I should pay attention too. I turn my head back to the ice just in time to see Colby skating ahead of everyone else—I think it's called a breakaway. He easily shoots the puck into the net, sending the Phantom's goalie sprawling onto the ice as he dives, trying to block it. The game is now 4-3 with ten seconds left.

The fans jump up from their seats and cheer. Even I can't help but jump up and down, cheering for Colby's goal—and that I'm saved from sitting here any longer with Dexter. I owe Colby big time.

Everyone is sitting back down when I see Colby skating straight toward me. I think perhaps he's heading in Bruce's direction, since we're seated behind the net, but no. He comes to stand straight in front of me and makes direct eye contact. He's grinning at me, and then he blows me a kiss and winks. It's impossible not to grin back at him. He's such a dog. I realize I'm the only one in our section still standing. And now I'm grinning like a fool, too.

I glance down at Dexter, who looks very unhappy that Colby is blowing a kiss to his date in front of thousands of people. Colby keeps grinning, turning and finishing his victory lap. When I sit down, I notice everyone's faces are tilted upward, staring at the jumbotron. Footage of Colby blowing me a kiss plays on repeat with Six Pence None the Richer's

Kiss Me playing loudly over the speakers. I blush so furiously I feel hot all over. I must be redder than an Eagle's jersey.

The Eagles win the game, then Dexter drives me home, barely speaking during the drive. The situation would usually send me spiraling into self-doubt, wondering what I did wrong, and over-analyzing everything I said during the date. But I'm on a high from Colby's attention. I'm on cloud nine from a kiss that was blown at me through plexiglass, a kiss that didn't even touch me. That's the power of Colby Knight's kisses. They can be felt, and even savored, even without any contact.

───────

I wake up the next morning to an overwhelming number of notifications on my phone. At first, I'm confused and think something must be wrong. But then I remember last night; a famous hockey player, a blown kiss, my face on the jumbotron.

I open the group message from Mel and Andie first.

MEL

OMG HE BLEW YOU A KISS.

ANDIE

That was the hottest no-contact kiss I've ever seen.

MEL

And you didn't seem too unhappy about it.

ANDIE

Totes agree.

ANDIE

PS How was your date? He didn't look as thrilled last night as you did.

I grimace at that last text. Poor Dexter, I feel bad for him. He's not a bad guy, just wrong for me. And now things will be awkward at work. Thankfully, I only see him in passing.

I have missed texts from my sister, Gram, my brothers, and Colby, along with a bunch of Google notifications. That's what I get for turning on Google notifications for Colby Knight. Feeling overwhelmed in knowing I'm the subject of so many people's conversations and criticisms makes my stomach bottom out. I sit up in my bed, resting against my headboard. A cold sweat breaks out on my forehead. I hate that I care what people are saying about me, the assumptions they must be making. The comments on photos that probably say, "Ew, why her? She's not even that pretty. He could do better."

I choose not to read any of the internet comments, for my own mental health.

With a deep breath, I read Colby's texts. Because Colby puts that piece of my brain at ease, the part that tells me I'm not good enough. He makes me feel really good, desired even.

COLBY

How was your date?

I snort an undignified laugh. He's so cheeky.

NOEL

It was okay, except he dragged me to some kind of aggressive, figure skating competition.

COLBY

Were there at least some hot guys for you to look at?

I laugh, then realize I've been grinning at my phone since I read Colby's first text. He makes me forget the haters, makes me not even care about them.

NOEL

There was a blond one guarding a big net. He was pretty cute.

COLBY

glaring emoji

COLBY

So, did your team win at least?

NOEL

Not sure, wasn't paying attention. I just hope they all had fun.

COLBY

GIF of Judge Judy palming her face in frustration

COLBY

It was great to see you there. Made me play better.

NOEL

I'm not sure Dexter enjoyed your antics.

COLBY

But it made you look desirable, even more so than normal. *wink emoji* I helped you out. You're welcome.

My stomach does another flip, but not in a good way. Was he only blowing me a kiss purely to help me win Dexter? Maybe I was right, maybe he's just a flirt and what I thought was a genuine connection was simply Colby being Colby. The thought hurts more than it should. I've guarded myself, I've been so careful, not wanting to get my heart broken again. I'm not sure when it happened, but sometime in the past month, I handed this man the power to crush me.

COLBY

And hey, you're famous now!

I swallow to clear the thick feeling in my throat, and blink rapidly to stop the tears from falling. He didn't mean to hurt me, he was helping. He thinks Dexter is the man of my dreams. I can't even be mad at him. It's all my fault for catching feelings. I steady myself and send him a text that I hope sounds like normal Noel, and not crushed Noel.

NOEL

Great, just what I wanted. *Tongue sticking out emoji*

I tap on the screen to get back into my group chat with the girls.

NOEL

Emergency tea sesh this morning?

MEL

Be there in an hour.

ANDIE

Me too.

CHAPTER 24
NOEL

MEL AND ANDIE are in my living room less than an hour later. We all have freshly brewed coffee and tea in our hands, even though I can't stomach the smell or taste of coffee at the moment.

"What's going on? Is it the online comments?" Mel asks, setting her tea down on the small table nearby. "I know they're harsh, but people are bored and have nothing better to do than comment on random stuff."

I've been vigilant about staying off the internet, but now I'm too curious to refrain any longer. I plunk my mug down on the side table and rush to my office to get my laptop. By the time I'm back in the living room, I've already Googled my own name and am reading through comments on a stalker-level Colby Knight fan account. They even have photos of us bungee jumping during my *evening with an Eagle*. Photos I never even cared enough about, until now, to look up.

I start reading through the comments on that first, gasping at one from PuckBunny69. I read it aloud to the girls, "Colby could have any girl he wants, and he's hanging out with this limp string-bean?"

Andie jumps up from her chair, half spilling her coffee in the process. She lunges, trying to grab the laptop from me. I yank it away and keep reading.

"MrsKnight27 says, 'He should've just dropped her off the platform and let her fall to her death.'"

Mel and Andie gasp. "Damn, that's heartless," Andie says.

"This might be even worse than the article that came out about you and Mitch," Mel tells her with wide eyes.

Back in the spring, Mitch was suspended and had to coach her brother's hockey team to rebuild his image. When they got together, an article came out accusing her of sleeping with her brother's coach to earn special favors. The whole thing almost caused them to break up.

I'm on a roll now, so I read the next comment too, "Colbys-Mistress<3 says, SpongeBob SquarePants has more curves than this girl. I give it one week before he leaves her for someone else."

I scroll down to a photo of Colby blowing me a kiss last night, a moment that felt so special to me. The first comment reads, *big deal, Colby has kissed half the women in D.C.* Another person replied to this comment saying, *AND slept with the other half.*

I don't read these out loud.

My hands go limp, and Andie gently removes the laptop from my fingers. "I think that's enough internet for today," she says.

Mel gets up and wraps me in a hug. "It's okay, people are mean when they're jealous."

I scoff. "They have nothing to be jealous of. Colby only blew me a kiss to make me look desirable in front of Dexter or something." I pull out of her arms and flop back onto my couch.

"Isn't that what you wanted?" Andie asks, her voice hesitant.

I sit up and drag my hands down my face. Conflicted about sharing all of my deepest, darkest thoughts and feelings. "Well, yeah. That's how it started. But I've been spending so much time with Colby and getting to know him. And he's wonderful."

Their faces soften at my confession, and I continue, "he's sweet, and funny, and thoughtful. And have you seen him? He wore a sweater-vest to one of our practice dates, and I almost swooned on sight. A sweater-vest has no business looking that hot!"

"So, once you got to know him, you started falling?" Mel eyes me with compassion.

I don't answer. Because we all know I'm falling for him. The entire nation. Because it's written all over my face in the kiss-blowing photos.

"And what about Dexter?" Andie asks, picking up her coffee and taking a sip. I get the feeling she's trying to hide a smile, like she knew I'd forget all about Dexter once I got to know Colby.

I sigh. "Dexter will be a great guy for some girl out there. Someone who loves British accents and philosophy."

The girls start laughing and so do I. My heart lifts, knowing these two are here for me no matter what. No judgment that I've been all over the place, not knowing what I wanted. But people change their minds, and sometimes life takes trial and error. We're allowed to grow and change to ebb and flow. And if I can give myself grace, then I need to extend that to Colby too. He's not who he used to be. He doesn't want to hurt me, or anyone. I can't hold his past against him. And I can't compare him to Travis.

But there's still that niggling feeling in the back of my mind that wonders if he really wants me. Or is he just flirting to flirt? Because his heart might not be as caught up in this as mine is. Leaning forward in my seat, I ask the girls, "do you think he even likes me though?"

Mel slinks back in her seat with a dramatic groan and Andie yells, "are you kidding me?!"

"You are so blind," Mel says with an eyeroll.

"The man is totally smitten with you!" Andie agrees, still half-shouting.

I wave them off. "Flirting with me and falling for me are two vastly different things."

"West told me he hasn't seen Colby with a woman in a year," Mel tells us with raised eyebrows.

"Mitch said the same," Andie nods her head so fast her hair gets in her eyes then looks at Mel. "I'd say between his recent celibacy and taking her to Pancake Palace, Colby must be pretty serious about our girl."

"Totally agree!" Mel says back.

"I'm sitting right here, guys."

Their heads snap over to stare at me. "Are you hearing the words coming out of our mouths, though? Are you going to stop doubting yourself and keep listening to random, bitter women on the internet?" Andie asks.

"Or are you going to go get your man?" Mel says, both of them staring me down.

A smile tugs at my lips. "Maybe it's time for one more practice date."

Mel's shoulders slump, thinking they didn't get their point across. "Practice date?"

"Yeah. I need practice kissing. Not sure I'm any good at it." I roll my lips together to keep from smiling.

Grinning, they nod their heads conspiratorially. Andie takes her thumb and forefinger and rubs her chin with an evil glint in her eye. "Great plan," she says. "I'm sure Colby would be happy to teach you."

CHAPTER 25
COLBY

I'M at the rink on Sunday for a long training day. First, we're working with our power play coach, then we'll work with our trainers in the gym. Last, we'll have massages and visit the team's physical therapists if needed. Then tomorrow we leave at the ass-crack of dawn for an away game and won't get back home until like three o'clock in the morning.

And that leaves very little time for me to see Noel.

Which is annoying, because she texted me last night wanting to do one more practice date. I'll take any date with her I can, even if it's practice for stupid Dexter. I was disappointed when she asked for another practice date, because that means she must still be into Dexter. Which means their date must've gone better than she let on.

And I hate that.

I should've never let her think me blowing her a kiss at the game was for his benefit. I should've been honest and told her I'm crazy about her. Told her to pick me. Love me. Kiss *me*.

I get through practice somehow, barely remembering any of my movements or what our power play coach said to us.

I walk into the team's cafeteria for lunch before our next

workout. Cafeteria makes it sound plain and juvenile, but it's a gourmet set up. It looks like a casual restaurant with rectangular tables and sturdy chairs. Everything is navy and red and embedded with the Eagles' logo. A buffet that smells amazing lines one whole wall of the room. I can smell the meal our nutritionist prepped for us, and it makes my mouth water. Our meals are always prepared for us when we have long training days like today, and also before evening games. And as much as I love my mother's Italian cooking, I always look forward to what Suzie makes for us. It's always healthy, with lots of protein and veggies to encourage our best performance. I get my food, filling two plates. I see Mitch and West already seated at a table, they're huddled together whispering, and when I come up behind them and take a seat, they both jump.

"Oh, hey Colby," West says, rubbing the back of his neck and avoiding eye contact.

Mitch is smirking. At least for him it's a smirk. The corner of his mouth twitching subtly. "Good practice," he grunts out.

"Uh, right," I say, looking between the two of them. "What were you guys talking about?"

"Nothing," they both say a little too quickly.

"You two are being weird," Remy says from behind me. None of us realized he'd walked up to us. Remy quirks a brow, then turns and stalks off toward the food.

I poke several pieces of lettuce with my fork and take a bite. "You're going to start keeping secrets from me now?" I ask with my mouth full, directing the question to West. "I thought we were besties."

West sighs. "I'm afraid we're honor bound to secrecy on this. Husband stuff."

"And fiancé." Mitch nods. "But it's nothing bad, it's good actually. And that's all I'm saying."

West chuckles under his breath. It's almost a giggle. Mitch

must kick him under the table because he flinches and levels Mitch with a glare.

Remy comes back to the table with a plate of food and sits down across from us. "Is this about the infamous kiss-blowing thing?"

West motions with a hand across his mouth like he's zipping it.

Remy rolls his eyes and starts eating. Bruce, who's always the last one to get his gear off—probably because he has twice as much padding to remove than the rest of us—joins us. He takes a seat beside Remy. Bruce grins, setting his plate down on the table. "Were you guys telling him that Noel wants kissing lessons?"

"Bruce!" Mitch and West yell in unison.

Remy's eyes go wide, almost as wide as mine. "She wants kissing lessons… from Colby?"

"Oops," Bruce says. "Was I not supposed to say anything?"

"Of course not, you asshat," Mitch grumbles.

Remy swallows the bite in his mouth and takes a big drink of his water. "Hey, this makes things easy for you. Another thing to check off your list."

"Yeah, I guess so." I look down at my food. "She only wants the practice to kiss *him*. I might get to kiss her, but he's the one who will get the real thing. He'll get to kiss her forever, and I'll get to kiss her *once*. And it won't be enough, not ever."

"Damn." Bruce gazes at me in awe. "You're completely gone for this girl."

I throw my hands up. "I've been telling you this for ages!"

West puts an arm around my shoulder. "I think everything will work out, man. Just wait and see."

I try to let his comment sink in, to give me some hope, but it's beginning to feel like she'll never be mine.

"By the way, Mel got the information you requested. About

FLIRTATION OR FACEOFF   193

guest appearances on campus," West says with a grin. "And it's a go."

Finally, something to lift my spirits today. I grin back at him, then look around the table at the guys. "Everyone free Tuesday? We're going back to school."

CHAPTER 26
NOEL

I'M late to my lecture. I'm *never* late. I'm always thirty minutes early. Prepped, polished and unwrinkled.

Not today.

I went to the on campus coffee shop for my daily over-priced, sugary beverage, only to run smack into Dexter and spill said beverage all over both of us. Dexter, who now calls me Dr. Woodcock again, simply had to strip off his damp sweater vest. His button-down dress shirt underneath was completely dry.

Unlike my very white, very sheer linen top. This was my favorite, and I don't know if I'll ever get this giant brown, coffee stain out. After spending thirty minutes under a hand-dryer in the restroom, my top is dry, but still looks disgusting. *And* I'm late.

I walk into the lecture hall, prickling with irritation and hating my unkempt appearance. The students take in my rumpled shirt with wide eyes and giggle quietly. I close my eyes and compose myself. What do I care if a bunch of nine-teen-year-olds think I'm a dork for spilling coffee. It happens to everyone.

Straightening my spine, I start going into my monologue about Mary, Queen of Scots, when I spot movement in the front row. My eyes widen so wide they probably look like Barbie doll eyes. Not one, but five enormous–and very familiar–men are seated in the front row with the most innocent expressions I've ever seen. It takes everything inside of me to stay calm. Not just because I have no idea why Colby is here in my class—along with West, Mitch, Remy, and Bruce—but because having Colby's gorgeous blue eyes on me is unnerving. And I missed him. I missed him so much that I hate hockey even more now. Because since the season kicked off, I've barely seen him. But here he is.

I allow myself a deep breath, before moving my eyes away from the giant hockey players and settling back into my lecture.

I almost lose it when I see the two hockey boys, that are always trying to get out of work, staring at the guys, their eyes filled with awe. They've never focused on one of my lectures this intently, if they did, they'd get straight A's in this class. They're practically drooling over the professional hockey players in the front row. I'm honestly embarrassed for them.

I glance at Colby and his teammates more times than I care to admit during my hour and a half long lecture and slideshow. (Which seemed like four hours.) And when they pulled notebooks and pens out of their backpacks? I almost died.

Where they found Lisa Frank school supplies, I have no idea. But it definitely takes me back to my childhood. Pretty sure I dreamt in Lisa Frank colors for the first twenty years of my life. Sparkly rainbow dolphins? Yes, please.

The guys were impressively studious, taking notes better than any student to ever come through my class before. Except Bruce, he was doodling photos of Mitch with no shirt on.

Which Mitch did not appreciate, if the few growls I heard are any indication.

I'm wrapping up my lecture right on time and dismiss my students. All the girls giggle and ogle my friends as they pass by. The two hockey scholarship kids are the last to leave, coming up to Colby and his teammates with stars in their eyes.

The blond one is breathing heavy when he says, "This is unreal! We're huge fans."

The darker-haired one sticks his hand out to Remy, probably hoping for a handshake. Colby, Remy, West, Mitch, and Bruce all stare at them, completely emotionless. Colby gives me a look, one eyebrow raises as if to ask, *are these the kids you told me about?*

Pulling my bottom lip in between my teeth, I nod, trying to hide my grin. So, this is why they came.

"I heard you're giving my girl, Noel, here some trouble." He clears his throat. "Sorry, my girl, Dr. Woodcock."

Both boys' eyes widen, and they glance at each other with panicked expressions. "No, sir. Of course not!" The blond one defends.

All five guys cross their arms at the same time, standing from their seats to stare down at the boys. "Dr. Woodcock is our favorite teacher!" the other one says, his voice cracking like he's about to cry.

"Is that right?" Colby asks. "You realize how important it is to take your studies seriously? To work your hardest?"

Bruce weighs in, being serious for once. "I worked my tail off in college before getting drafted. And that was a cake walk compared to playing in the NHL."

Mitch grunts. "We're always working. Between games, training, and media nonsense."

West nudges him in the side, probably warning him to watch his language. "We love it, and we're grateful we get to do what we love. But consider college a part of your training, training in hard work and perseverance."

Remy steps forward one intimidating step. "And always respect the people who have your best interest at heart. Such as your professors."

The boys swallow, still looking terrified, they both mumble *yes sir.*

All five giant hockey players relax their shoulders and smile, even Mitch. I can tell they practiced this whole thing, which makes me giddy in a way I can't explain. I feel... rescued. And it's obvious which one of them orchestrated this entire intervention. Colby pulls a black, permanent marker out of his backpack. "Okay, now do you want our signatures?"

The boys nod emphatically, finally relaxing into easy smiles.

When the hockey boys turn to leave the lecture hall, everything they're wearing has signatures on it. Their sweatshirts, hats, jeans. They look elated.

The dark-haired one turns to me before he reaches the door. "We'll start working harder, Dr. Woodcock. Promise."

The blond one gives me a genuine smile. "We'll even join the study group to get our grades up."

"Good. Happy to hear it." I smile back and they exit, closing the door behind them.

The six of us burst into laughter the moment the door clicks. "How did you guys find my classroom?"

West shrugs. "Mel may have helped."

"Of course, she did. And the Lisa Frank notebooks? Nice touch."

"Andie had a bunch of them from when she was a kid," Mitch adds, acting bashful about the whole thing.

As if someone would think this giant of a man was somehow less masculine because he touched a pink notebook with a purple sea turtle on the cover. All five of them ooze masculinity in a way I've never seen before. The whole tough, strong, sexy hockey player thing is certainly working for them. Especially Colby. But there's something softer about him than the others. He's sweeter, not as rough around the edges. I can picture him holding a baby, or baking cupcakes, playing Barbies with his little sister, or even being a cat dad. I don't know how I didn't notice this before, other than I chose not to notice, because I didn't want to. Because I wanted to protect myself. I never wanted to fall for another playboy-athlete.

But Colby is much more than that.

He's a person who brings people together. He's someone who can host an impromptu BBQ between two families who are total opposites and who've never met before. He's a man who can, despite traveling for an away game, wrangle all of his teammates into sticking up for a friend. He's a friend who's always caring for those he loves and thinking of ways to make them smile.

And what I wouldn't give to be that. To be someone he loves.

I realize I'm staring at Colby, probably with hero-worship written all over my face. Colby's teammates glance between the two of us, mumbling about how they'll meet him in the car.

When it's just Colby and I left in the lecture hall, the silence is thick. Our breathing is in sync, our chests rising and falling with every second that passes by.

"So," I finally say. "You're back from your trip?"

His hand flexes at his side, and I wonder if it's because he wants to touch me as badly as I want to touch him. I hope that's the reason. "Yeah. We won." He grins. "Hey, are you free for dinner? We could grab dinner at Pancake Palace and discuss your... lessons." He swallows on the last word and his voice goes all deep and raspy. "You mentioned you needed one more?"

"Yeah, I need help with something." My face goes hot. "Pancake Palace tonight sounds good." I clear my throat, since it's suddenly feeling thick. "Will it be... private? Like last time?"

He nods. "Yeah, the manager always clears the main room for me. I already reserved my booth a week ago. I'm always hungry for pancakes after an away game."

I chuckle. "Why doesn't that surprise me?"

CHAPTER 27
COLBY

WALKING up to my teammates in the University parking lot, they're all resting against my G-wagon and grinning.

"Dude!" Bruce shouts. "She was staring at you like she wanted to rip your clothes off."

I wrinkle my nose. "Show a little respect."

He straightens up, smiling apologetically. But his words secretly bolster me. Because I totally thought she was looking at me like she wanted to rip my clothes off, but I thought maybe it was all in my head.

"But honestly... we could've cut the sexual tension with a knife," West says with raised eyebrows. "I think our gameplan is working."

"If Noel is falling for me, you guys don't get *any* of the credit."

"The game plan has made my gym wall look like trash for a month. So, I think I, at least, get some credit," Remy adds, sticking his hands in the pockets of his jeans.

Mitch groans loudly and rolls his eyes. "Can we go now? I'm exhausted and I have a gorgeous woman waiting to take a nap with me."

"Napping? Is that what you kids are calling it these days?" Bruce jests, earning a glare from Mitch.

West pats Mitch on the back, hard. "I'm with Mitch on this one."

We pile into my G-wagon, and I drive them back to the iceplex where we met up before driving to Arlington University. On the drive back, we're all quiet, probably from exhaustion due to traveling all night. Private plane or not, we're still tired. In the silence, I think about Mitch and West, heading home to Mel and Andie. How nice it must be to have someone home waiting for you. How comforting it must be to slip into a warm bed and curl up next to your partner. I allow myself to picture coming home to Noel, her in my bed. In my daydream she's reading a book and her eyes are sleepy because she stayed up too late reading. She has a stack of books on the nightstand, and a few bookmarks scattered around. She's wearing classic silk button-down pajamas. They're white and angelic, maybe with little pink polka dots.

Definitely with little pink polka dots. A slow grin spreads across my face and I don't even realize that I'm smiling like a total weirdo until Bruce, who's in the front seat, snickers. "You're totally thinking about Noel right now, aren't you?"

I punch his arm, hard. "No. I wasn't."

He's undeterred. "Hmm." He rubs his chin thoughtfully. "Lemme guess, you're picturing her pencil skirt and heels— being all hot and professor-y?"

"Shut up, Bruce," we all say in unison with a groan.

———

I arrive early to Pancake Palace, and as usual, Todd has the area with my favorite booth closed off for privacy. Two words keep racing through my mind over and over again: kissing lessons.

My palms are sweaty, like a teenager on his first date. I've never been this nervous in my life. Part of my strange mood has nothing to do with kissing her, but wondering why she thinks she needs lessons in that area. Has she never been kissed before? Or has she, and some asshole made her feel like she didn't do it well?

Either way, it's a lot of pressure. And then there's the pang of jealousy in my gut that she wants to be a good kisser for Dr. Dickhead. Ugh.

I'm so wrapped up in my thoughts, I don't notice how much time has passed. Footsteps draw my attention, and I look up to see Noel. My angel.

She's wearing silky, cream-colored pants with black pointed toe flats. The pants come up high on her waist and have pleats in the front. But with her fitted black top tucked into them, she pulls off the outfit. You'd think the ensemble would appear masculine, but it oozes femininity.

Since when do words like *femininity* pop into my head? I guess all the books I've been reading lately have already expanded my vocabulary.

I glance down at what I'm wearing, not even remembering what I put on. Black wash jeans, and a pale green Henley. I don't look as good as Noel, but this shirt hugs my chest, so I think it'll be okay.

Noel slides into the booth and smiles at me. Her cheeks are flushed, and I wonder if she's nervous, too. She slides close to me; much closer than the first time I brought her here. I smile at her, thinking of how far we've come in only a few weeks. We're friends now, we talk all the time, we hang out... and she smiles at me in that familiar way. A smile that says, *Hey, I know you and I enjoy being around you.*

"I thought the professor look was hot, but these trousers really take the cake," I say, breaking the silence.

She rolls her eyes at me the way she always does, but she's trying to hide a smile. "I still can't believe you guys sat in on my class after you traveled all night."

"Angel, I'd do anything for you. Night or day. No matter how exhausted I was." It comes out of my mouth before I can censor it or play it off as a joke or silly flirting.

Her eyes widen, but she doesn't look away. I study the color of her eyes again, those circles of caramel, or of coffee, with the perfect amount of creamer. I could stare into them all night.

"So," she breaks the silence. "Buffet?"

"Ladies first." I gesture toward the twenty-four-hour breakfast buffet with a flourish of my hand.

She scoots back out of the booth and floats across the yellow floor with that graceful walk of hers. I won't lie—I check out her butt. Those pants are incredible all around.

Noel loads up her plate the way she did last time, as do I, then we head back to our booth. *Our* booth. This place is no longer reserved for just me. It's ours now, whether she knows it or not. Whatever happens, or doesn't happen, between us, I'll never be able to come here without picturing her here beside me.

Todd brings out a coffee carafe and the little tubs of my favorite cinnamon creamer, smiles, and leaves us without a word.

Silence between us is usually comfortable, but as we eat, it seems tense and weird. I miss annoying her and the jabs she shot back at me. I miss our easy banter and how she's never afraid to give me hell. I have the urge to rile her up, to ruffle her feathers and break the strange awkwardness.

"You're in need of more of my expertise to snag Dr. what's-his-face, huh? Couldn't seal the deal the other night?"

She lifts her chin defiantly, and her eyebrows scrunch. "Yeah, well, your silly kiss-blowing made him mad instead of making me desirable. So maybe you shouldn't have put on a show."

She's annoyed, but at least she's not silently staring down at her pancakes.

"If he got mad over a silly kiss blown through plexiglass, then he must not be very confident. He could've taken charge and kissed you himself." I stare into her eyes. "Or *did* he kiss you?" My heart is in my throat, waiting for her answer.

"Not yet," she says, her jaw tense. "But he will." Something flickers in her eyes that makes me think she's lying.

"If you're so sure, then what is tonight's lesson about?" I ask, leaning closer, daring her to tell me what she truly wants. Because the way she's staring at me, all hot and annoyed, doesn't tell me she's thinking about some other guy.

Her breaths are coming faster, and her eyes drop briefly to my mouth. She bites her bottom lip, looking unsure.

Don't back down now, tell me what you want, I silently urge.

"I need you to show me how to kiss," the words rush out of her mouth, like she has to say them before she changes her mind. "I'm not any good."

Two emotions are at war in my mind; wanting to beat the shit out of the man who made her feel this way. And excitement, because I desperately want to kiss her.

"Your ex made you feel like you were a bad kisser?"

She huffs a humorless laugh. "I've never kissed anyone but him. So, yeah."

My eyes drop down to her mouth, a pouty bottom lip paired with a perfect cupid's bow on top. Then I look back up at her eyes, still full of fire and sass. "Angel, that's not possible.

You have more passion in one pinky finger than some people have in their entire body." I inch a little closer. "Maybe you just weren't kissing the right guy."

She swallows slowly, her eyes not leaving mine. "I don't know. I don't think lessons would hurt."

I bite the insides of my cheeks to keep from smiling. This woman.

Leaning my head down slowly, I give her the chance to change her mind. But she leans in also, her lips are parted and I can feel her breath on my mouth. We're literally a breath away from each other. If either of us moved even a millimeter, our lips would brush together.

She pulls back slightly, gazing up at me. "What's the matter? Worried you won't live up to the hype?"

The challenge in her voice is all it takes for me to press my mouth to hers, hard. Since she thinks she can't kiss, I probably should've started slow, with just a peck. But she doesn't skip a beat, pressing into my lips with all the passion I knew she was capable of.

I slide my hand up to her neck, gently pressing my palm into the warm, soft skin there. Then I move my hand up to cup her jaw, wanting to touch and memorize every inch of her. Everything about her is sweet, from her sugar cookie scent to her lips that still taste faintly of pancake syrup.

Slanting my head to the side, I part her lips with my own, savoring the pressure of our mouths tangling together. Bringing my other hand up, I cup her face in my palms, angling her head and her mouth right where I need them, giving her the kiss she deserves.

When she finally pulls back to look at me, her lips are pink and swollen, visible proof of our kisses. It makes me want to lean back in and kiss her again.

"Your ex was an idiot," I whisper, slowly dropping my

hands from her face to her legs, where I allow them to rest on her knees.

Her head falls back, and she releases the most brilliant laugh I've ever heard. "You think so?" she asks.

"I think he's the one who needed kissing lessons."

She laughs again, then sobers. "Colby, I don't want to kiss Dexter."

The way my heart leaps at those words should be embarrassing. I squeeze her knees with my hands, wanting to keep touching her and trying to hold back. "You don't?"

She quirks her lips to the side. "No."

"Good," I say seriously, reaching up to tuck one of her blonde curls behind her ear. "Don't kiss Dexter. Don't kiss anyone but me, Noel. Please."

She shakes her head, not breaking eye contact. "I don't want to kiss anyone but you." She pauses. "And you're sure I'm not a bad kisser?"

I ignore her question and kiss her again.

CHAPTER 28
NOEL

WOW. I thought I'd been kissed before, but whatever is happening right now is completely erasing every kiss from Travis from my memory. Colby's lips have magical, memory-erasing powers. All I want to do is yank his face back down and kiss him again and again. I've never had this frenzy of sensation before. This is what all my books are talking about... the chemistry between both main characters, the undeniable pull to one another.

Colby pulls back, his eyes dilated in a way that tells me he'd like to keep this up. But we have to talk about this. We can't simply make out and go back to eating our pancakes, then leave Pancake Palace. Like, *bye, thanks for the tongue action, buddy.*

"When you blew me a kiss, was it honestly just for show?" I ask before I can chicken out.

He laughs, still sounding breathless. "Of course not. I wanted to jump over the glass and kiss you in front of everyone. Every time I see you, I want to touch you, kiss you." His eyes dip down to his lap, his usual confident demeanor slipping. "Noel, I just want you to be *mine*, damn it."

A watery laugh slips out and I slip my hand into his. "I'm sorry it took me so long to see it, to see how good we could be. But Colby, I think I'd like to be yours."

The way his face lights up at my admission makes me fall a little harder. He takes my hand in his, his expression sobering. "What about Dexter?"

"Our date was truly horrible," I admit. Colby grins and I give him a playful push. "And my heart wasn't in it from the start. You crashed into my world like a literal wrecking ball. Miley Cyrus would be proud."

He laughs at my joke, then I continue, "I've thought about you constantly since the charity auction. The way it felt to dance with you, the way you drive me crazy. And how annoyingly confident you are." I groan. "You even ruined sweater vests for me!"

Colby breaks into a full-on laugh at this. "You were into that, huh? I knew you would be. You little freak." He winks, and I roll my eyes.

Colby's expression grows serious, and he absently rubs the back of my hand with his thumb. "Where do we go from here?"

"Can we just keep doing what we've been doing?" I ask. "But with more kissing?"

"I think that's called dating," Colby says slowly, a smile spreading across his face, showing off those magnificent dimples.

"I'm aware," I tease. "But can we take things slow? My last relationship ended horribly. I never thought I'd recover. And it's hard for me to trust because of it."

He nods. "We can go slow. You set the pace. And I know I'll need to keep earning your trust. I know I have a past, but I need you to know I would never, ever cheat on someone. After watching my mother go through that, I could never treat another person that way. Your well-being... your *heart*... is important to me."

"Thank you." My voice is thick with emotion. "I think I needed to hear that."

"Another thing you should know," he says carefully. "Never believe everything you read online. And stay away from comment sections."

"I'm afraid you're too late. PuckBunny69 already put me in my place."

"Who?" he asks, his brow furrowing adorably in confusion. "Nevermind."

———

I could have talked to, and kissed, Colby all night.

We sit in the sticky, yellow booth for hours, but I have early classes tomorrow.

Once I'm back home, alone in my apartment and showered with my jammies on, my bed suddenly feels way too big for only myself. The air is growing colder at night now that it's October, and I bet Colby would keep the blankets so warm. With his big muscular body and skin that always seems hot to the touch.

I reach over for my cord to plug my phone in, seeing I have missed texts from the girls. I laugh through my nose; I should've expected this.

MEL
So? How'd it go?

ANDIE
Yeah, we need details on your kissing lesson!

MEL

Maybe they're still kissing?

ANDIE

He had to give her a VERY thorough lesson. *wink emoji*

MEL

Okay, it's been like four hours, Noel!

ANDIE

You have to come up for air eventually!

I chuckle to myself as I type out a response.

NOEL

Wow, sorry girls. The kissing lesson was quite educational. I think my skills have grown immensely.

ANDIE

But the real question is... will you need more than one lesson?

MEL

Or did one lesson do the trick?

I know what they're really asking. They want to know if we talked about our feelings, if we're going to keep seeing each other without the ruse of Colby being my dating coach.

NOEL

Colby has agreed to continue my lessons for as long as I'd like. I think I'll need them for a very long time.

MEL

GIF of Monica, Rachel, and Phoebe jumping up and down

ANDIE

GIF of Michael Scott and Dwight raising the roof

MEL

This makes me ridiculously happy.

ANDIE

Me too! And now you HAVE to come to the game with us on Friday.

NOEL

Oh yeah, I guess I should probably watch hockey now, huh?

ANDIE

Girl, you know I don't go to games for the hockey. I go to stare at Mitch.

MEL

I love hockey, watching West is just an added bonus.

NOEL

Okay. I can manage staring at Colby for an evening, I guess.

CHAPTER 29
COLBY

COACH YOUNG WAS KIND ENOUGH to allow an afternoon practice the day after we got back from our away game. We all needed to catch up on sleep, Coach included. Not that I got much sleep after that kiss.

If I thought about Noel Woodcock a lot before, it's even worse now. My need for her ignited beyond reason. I was too excited to sleep last night and finally turned my lamp on and finished The Fellowship of the Ring. Now I know why chicks are obsessed with Aragorn. The dude is a stud.

I enter the locker room, still daydreaming about Noel, and almost slam right into the new defenseman, the one that's been out with a minor injury, Travis Evander. He's all suited up and wearing a full contact jersey, his reddish-brown hair peeking out from under his helmet.

"Hey! Watch where you're going," he grits out, his brow furrowed in an annoyed way.

I'm almost the same height as him even though he's wearing skates and I'm not—he must be barely 5'10".

When he sees me and realizes who I am, he huffs a laugh, trying to back track. "Oh, sorry Knight. Didn't realize it was you. I thought the equipment manager was back with the wrong gloves again." He rolls his eyes.

"Jim is great. He's never gotten my gear mixed up all the years I've been with the Eagles. A little respect goes a long way. Doesn't matter if it's the general manager, or the social media manager. We're all part of a team here," I tell him earnestly.

Jim is the most organized person I know, but some players are total divas and are never happy.

"Right, I'll remember that." He appears slightly embarrassed.

"Glad to see you're in full contact today. We need your defensive skills."

"Me too, man," he says tersely, a tick in his jaw. "See ya on the ice." Travis brushes past me.

Something about the guy sets off my douchebag meter. I can't put my finger on what exactly it is. Just a vibe I'm getting, and that he was talking crap about Jim. Hopefully I'm wrong, because his defensive skills are exactly what we need to help us win the cup.

I walk into the locker room where everyone is putting on their gear and their skates. Jim comes in behind me. He smiles and says good morning before dropping off three different sizes of gloves at the station with Travis's name on it. Three of the walls in our locker room are lined with large cubbies where we store our gear, and we each have a name plate. It's similar to preschool cubby, but fancier. I turn and find Remy and West talking quietly in the corner of the room.

"Why does everyone have so many secrets these days?" I ask, placing one arm around each of their shoulders.

Remy sighs heavily. "The new defenseman that they pulled from the AHL is a drama queen."

West nods in agreement, then grins. "So? What happened last night?"

I release them, stepping toward my cubby. "A gentleman never kisses and tells."

Bruce waddles up beside me in his full goalie gear, removing his mouth guard before saying, "Yeah, but you're not a gentleman."

Mitch walks into the locker room, taking a seat in front of his station, which is right next to mine. "Well, what happened? Did I miss it?"

We all stare at him and he shrugs. "You drug us into your mess and now I'm invested."

"Fair enough." I laugh. "Okay," I whisper. "I kissed her."

"Did you make sure it was a once in a lifetime kind of kiss?" Bruce asks.

I shove him and he almost topples over. "Those are the only kisses I'm capable of, doofus."

The guys laugh.

"That's great, man," Remy says, patting me once on the shoulder. It's a big statement coming from him, because he's not typically a touchy person.

"And is she done with Dr. Dickhead?" West asks, smiling knowingly. I'm sure Mel already filled him in on everything.

"She is." I grin, feeling on top of the world.

"Wow, I can't believe she doesn't hate you anymore. It's the end of an era, ya know?" Bruce muses, earning another shove. West catches him before he falls to the ground in all of his padding.

Remy claps his hands together. "Alright boys, get suited up. We need to get acquainted with our newest defenseman, and Mitch," he lowers his voice so only the four of us can hear him. "You're gonna have your work cut out for you with this one."

Mitch grunts. "If I can work with twelve-year-olds, I can handle Travis Evander."

Remy raises an eyebrow as if to say, *are you sure about that?*

CHAPTER 30
NOEL

IT'S ONLY BEEN two days since I saw Colby, and I miss him. It's honestly pathetic.

So, I was thrilled when he called me last night and asked if I was free this evening. It's one of the few nights he doesn't have a game or any other team events. When I asked what we were doing, all he told me was that he'd pick me up after I got home from work, around four.

We pull up to the D.C. Children's Hospital, the one the charity gala raised money for. I look down at what I'm wearing; black tights with a tiny floral print, leather slip-on shoes, and a simple brown sweaterdress. I'm not sure why we're here, but I can only assume I'm overdressed.

Colby reaches over and holds my hand, the warmth of his olive skin instantly soothing my worries and making me realize that it makes no difference if I'm overdressed. Or underdressed. No one cares. And if they do, it doesn't matter. I take a deep breath. "So, what are we doing here?"

He smiles. "This is one of the charities that the Eagles support. Which is why I was at the auction. Me and Bruce come visit the kids every month. We hand out toys and stickers and chat with the kids. It's my favorite community outreach opportunity."

I squeeze his hand. "Wow, that's amazing. I never realized sports teams are so involved in their communities."

"Most NHL teams are. They do a lot of good work." He pauses. "But I have to warn you, Bruce is mad at you for taking his place tonight."

I laugh. "Oh no, he's a scary guy."

Colby chuckles at that. "Best goalie in the NHL, but the *least* scary." He releases my hand, getting out of the vehicle and grabbing a big, Eagles' duffle bag before coming around to open my door for me. As soon as I'm standing, he's holding my hand again, like now that he has permission to touch me, he can't stop.

And I don't want him to. My heart swells that he wants to be near me, that he's sharing this special thing with me tonight. Taking me to help him with something that he enjoys. It feels like the beginning of a life together.

After checking into the hospital, getting our badges, and taking the elevator up, we come to the first room. There's a young boy in the hospital bed, surrounded by stuffed animals. He has an Eagles snow hat on his head and is hooked up to an I.V. My heart breaks at the sight. This precious, innocent child having to endure so much.

Colby knocks on the doorframe, causing the boy and his parents to glance up at us. Their faces light up at the sight of Colby as he strides inside the room before setting the black duffle bag on the ground.

Sitting on the boy's bed, he holds his fist out and the boy pounds it. "Hey man! I brought a friend today. This is Noel." Colby looks over at me and says, "Noel, this is my buddy, Broderick."

The little boy turns his big, brown eyes on me then whispers, "she's pretty."

Colby whispers back, "The prettiest."

Is someone squeezing my heart? Because that's what it feels like.

I walk over and introduce myself to the parents, then go to stand near Broderick. "It's really nice to meet you."

He peers up at me with a bashful glint in his eyes.

"Noel brought some extra special goodies, wanna see?" Colby asks him, then nods his head toward the bag.

Grabbing the bag, I set it on the bed and Broderick's eyes widen with excitement. I give Colby a secret smile, thanking him for helping me win Broderick over and make him more comfortable with my presence. Inside the bag are a bunch of soft pucks in a rainbow of colors. They look like you can squeeze them, similar to a stress ball. "What's your favorite color?" I ask.

He answers green and I hand him a bright green puck. He squeezes it with both hands. "These are so cool!"

We're all smiling as we watch him get excited over something seemingly small. "Have you been watching our games?" Colby asks him, making conversation easily, a skill he seems to have with people no matter the age.

"I haven't missed one yet!"

"Good," Colby nods. "You're our lucky charm, I think. We've won all three games so far."

Broderick grows serious. "I'll keep watching then."

For over an hour, I follow Colby from room to room, handing out pucks and watching him with the kids. He remembers all of their names, and things they enjoy. He even knows their parents and what they do. This is more to him than mandatory team participation. He genuinely cares about people. I'm not sure how it's possible, but in one evening it feels like my attraction to this man has grown by 100 percent.

I'm about to cry at how sweet he is or grab him and kiss his lips because I'm that drawn to him.

When we get back in his G-Wagon, he turns to gaze at me. "I was going to take you to a restaurant to eat, but I have another idea. And if it's too much, too soon, you can say no."

I tense, wondering what he's talking about. "Okay..."

"My mother and stepdad are at my house right now. I pay Ma to make my meals for the week and clean. She's an amazing cook. She's probably cooking up some homemade pasta and basil pesto as we speak." He huffs a laugh. "She's dying to meet you. Especially since my dad already did."

I don't even have to think about it. I want to meet her too. I want to know the woman who raised Colby, and I want to hug her. "Let's go meet her."

"Are you sure?" His eyebrows raise in surprise.

"Yeah, of course. Who else is going to show me your baby pictures?"

CHAPTER 31
COLBY

MA'S FACE brightens instantly when she looks up from her workstation in my kitchen and notices Noel beside me. The kitchen island is a disaster of flour and cooking supplies. It's always messy on the days she cooks. She has individual glass serving containers lined up and ready to fill with whatever she's cooking up. Once she fills the containers, she marks each one with what's inside like I'm ten, and I love her for it. I have to buy a few pre-made salads for the week though. Ma only knows how to cook carbohydrates. She wipes her hands on her apron, then uses them to smooth her hair self-consciously. My stepdad, Charlie, is at her side in the kitchen, stirring something on the stovetop. He turns quickly, making his silver hair fall into his eyes, and smiles. His dark brown eyes are bright as he takes us in.

I've never introduced them to a girl. Ever. I can practically see the wedding plans running through Ma's head. I take a few strides into the kitchen, pulling Noel by the hand. "Ma, Charlie, I'd like you to meet Noel."

Ma's eyes get shiny with unshed tears. Oh gosh, please

don't cry. She rushes forward and hugs Noel. "Oh, it's wonderful to meet you. I didn't think this day would ever come!"

She's practically strangling Noel. I pat Ma on the back, a silent urge to let go. She pulls back grinning so big it looks painful.

Charlie steps forward and takes Noel's hand. "Pleasure meeting you." Then he turns to glance at me. "And you, young man, have been so busy I've barely seen you lately!" Charlie pulls me into a big hug, feeling more like a father to me than my real one ever has.

I pull back, smiling. "You taking good care of Ma? I know she's a handful."

Charlie laughs as Ma pops me in the back of the head. "That is not true!" Her head swivels to look at Noel. "Don't believe a word he says."

Noel smiles, enjoying the exchange. "I've heard nothing but wonderful things. Mostly about your cooking."

Ma rolls her eyes. "Always thinking about food, this one." She pokes me in the stomach as if there's any fat there.

I swat her hand away. "I assumed you made a feast and there'd be enough for me and Noel to eat for dinner."

"Of course! Of course!" She eyes Noel for a moment. "You're not one of those types that eats like a rabbit, are you?"

Noel snorts a laugh and I answer for her. "Noel eats almost as much as I do."

Ma releases a deep breath. "Whew! Because I made garlic bread, fettuccini, and homemade pesto sauce."

"That sounds amazing," Noel says.

Ma grabs two of my nicest plates and whispers something to Charlie before turning toward me and Noel again. "So, tell me about yourself!"

Charlie adds food to the plates, arranging everything perfectly, like a restaurant would.

Noel blows out a small breath as she thinks. "I teach history at Arlington U. I'm from a small town in Maryland, which is where my family still lives. Except for my grandmother, she lives here in the city."

"Wonderful!" Ma says, grabbing two candles from under my sink and carrying them to the table and lighting them. "Do you have a big family?"

Noel smiles. "I do, three siblings."

"And do you want a big family?" Ma pries, her voice tight with excitement, and her eyes wide as if already picturing a dozen grandchildren.

"Ma!" I groan. "Enough with the interrogation."

Noel laughs and Ma throws her hands in the air. "What?" she says. "It's a normal question."

"No, it's not," Charlie says, pinning his wife with a serious expression.

Noel and I glance at each other and can barely contain our laughter.

Ma looks unamused as she turns and grabs napkins and silverware. Within five minutes my dining room table is set for a romantic date night, food included. Ma is a woman on a mission, apparently.

"Do you cook for Colby every week?" Noel asks.

Ma finally stops and rests against the kitchen counter. "I do." She smiles. "He bought me an apartment here when he signed with the Eagles, and I told him I'd do it to pay him back. But years later, he still pays me anyway."

Noel looks up at me, her eyes are soft. She doesn't appear bothered by my mother cooking for me even though I'm thirty, and that's a relief. I realize it could make me look like a huge mama's boy. But hopefully she knows me well enough by now to know that I simply enjoy taking care of the people I love. And before Charlie, Ma needed my help. *And* it's not exactly a burden since my house is always clean, and every week my fridge is full of homemade Italian food.

"Well, let us clean up and then we'll get out of your hair." Ma turns on the water and grabs the scrub brush for the dirty dishes and Charlie sidles up next to her.

"You guys don't have to rush off," I insist. "Stay a while and chat."

Ma widens her eyes at me, and I know that look. I can practically read her mind. She's silently urging me to spend time alone with Noel, to woo her.

I widen my eyes back as if to say *we have plenty of time to get to know each other.*

Ma purses her lips and raises one eyebrow. Her expression is conveying, *no you don't, you're already thirty.*

Noel and I sit down to eat while Charlie and Ma clean the kitchen up in record time. The kitchen is in view of the large dining table, so we awkwardly watch them do their speed clean.

"Something tells me your mother wants us to spend time alone," Noel whispers.

"She wants grandbabies," I whisper back.

Noel laughs, choking on the noodle she just put in her mouth.

Ma and Charlie make their way over to the table, the kitchen now pristine. "You two are adorable over here giggling," Ma gushes, patting me on the head.

Charlie shakes his head at the woman, but he has a fond smile on his face. "We're going to head out, glad I could finally see you, Colby, and lovely meeting you, Noel. We hope to see more of you in the future." He winks at Noel and her cheeks grow a shade darker.

Ma kisses the top of my head and says, "Non rovineare tutto, mio figlio." Which is *don't mess this up, my son,* in Italian. I'm not fluent like my mother, but I've heard this expressions enough over the years to understand it.

———

We finish dinner and I guide Noel to my living room. Not my fancy, staged living room that's right off the dining and kitchen area, but the one down the hallway. This one is cozy with an overstuffed sectional. Hockey memorabilia and framed jerseys line the walls. A giant flatscreen takes up one entire wall in front of the sofa, but it's one of those that can look like framed artwork when you want it to. Right now, there's a giant picture of the French countryside.

Noel grins as she studies the space. "Okay, this room looks like you. The rest of your house is so—"

"Boring?"

"Well, yes. I mean, it's gorgeous. But plainer than I'd expect for *the* Colby Knight," she admits.

I smile, plopping down on my comfortable sofa then patting the spot beside me. "Come here, I have something to show you."

She sits close to me, close enough that our thighs brush together. The awareness of her body touching mine almost makes me forget what I want to show her. She eyes me expectantly and I huff a laugh.

"Right." I reach over, grasping my copy of Fellowship of The Ring from the round coffee table and hand it to her.

Noel looks at it, flipping it over and seeing the tabs sticking

out of the pages. She gasps quietly. "Oh, my gosh. You annotated it?"

"Anno what?" I laugh. "I just highlighted things I enjoyed
and added tabs if there was a scene that really struck me."

She chuckles. "Yeah, that's annotating. And it's... really
sexy."

CHAPTER 32
NOEL

I'M STARING at his lips, I know I am. But how can I stop myself from kissing him when he not only read, but annotated, one of my favorite books ever. The fact that he took the time to read this simply because I like it does something to my heart. My chest feels tight, but also light at the same time. I want to go back in time and tell my twenty-year-old self to hold out for the guy who adores me enough to read my favorite book. Only so he could talk to me about it, and share something with me.

I've been holding back from Colby for far too long, trying to ignore the growing feelings and the undeniable attraction, and I don't want to fight it anymore. I lean in and press my mouth to his, the stubble of his five o'clock shadow brushes against my chin, heightening the sensation of his soft lips. His arms come up to my sides, then wrap around my waist. I feel safe here, so impossibly content, I could cry. It's something I've never had with anyone else.

Before I know what I'm doing, I slide one leg over his thighs, sitting on his lap facing him. A move I never would have thought myself sexy enough to pull off, or confident enough to try. But Colby's kiss bolsters me in a way nothing ever has.

Straddling his strong thighs gives me the closeness I'm craving, the direct access to his lips that I want. His arms tighten around my waist, pulling me into him. He's sturdy and solid, but also soft and warm. He's everything, filling all of my senses. The taste of his mouth on mine, sweet from the wine we drank. The smell of his skin, spicy like rum. The feel of his warm skin moving against mine. It's all too much, and not enough at the same time. My fingers slide into that silky, dark hair of his. I've wondered if his hair was as soft as it looked, and it is.

I'm desperate to get closer to him, but he gives me one long kiss before gently pulling away. I try to pull him back to me and he chuckles, a low, rumbly sound. I open my eyes to gaze at him, and even though he's smiling at me, his eyes are dark with want. He has the appearance of just waking up from a great dream, especially since his hair is all messy from my eager hands.

Gently, he rubs his large hands up and down my back.

I try once more to lean in and kiss him again, but he glides his hands up to my shoulders and pushes against me, stopping me from getting closer. I don't know why he's pushing me away, why he's holding back. But as always, he reads me like a book. Always knowing what my expression is saying.

"Angel, let's slow down."

"Why?"

He chuckles again but stops when he studies my face. Noting my offended expression. I move to get off his lap, feeling embarrassed by my boldness. Wondering why I was so forward, and also why he didn't like it.

He holds me in place by wrapping his arms around my waist again. "Hey, look at me."

My eyes obey his command before my brain can stop them.

"Do you know why I moved fast with girls in the past?"

When I don't answer, he continues, "because I wanted one night with them. That's it. One night and nothing else. Because I was a boy, not a man. Because I was young and careless, and I hurt people. I wasn't trying to, but I did." He closes his eyes as if the thought pains him. "But Noel, I want to do things right with you. Because I don't only want one night with you. I want forever."

Tears fill my eyes before running down my face. His words are so honest, so sweet. Colby's sapphire eyes are locked on mine, and I can tell he means every word just by the way he's looking at me. I think it's the way he's always looked at me, I was just too dumb to notice.

He brings his hands up to cup my face, then gently brushes my tears away with his thumbs. "What's wrong?"

I sniff. "What's wrong, is that I'm an idiot."

His lips pull up in a half-smile. "Why do you say that?"

"Because it took me so long to see how amazing you are."

He shoots me his infamous cocky grin, the one with the dimples. "It really did take way too long."

I laugh, leaning in so my forehead presses against his. "Forever sounds pretty good."

———

Friday night I pick Gram up for the game. When I told her about my failure of a date with Dexter—and then my kiss with Colby—she insisted on being my bodyguard to every home game from this point forward. Gram even claimed she'd, "take a ho down if they try to shank me for taking Colby Knight off the market."

We meet the girls at a special entrance where employees

and families can come in without being bombarded. The buzz around us is overwhelming. Tonight feels vastly different from the last game I came to. Now, I'm Colby Knight's... what, girlfriend? Girlfriend sounds like a childish term, but I suppose that's what I am. Will people be rooting for me and Colby? Or ripping us apart? I take a deep breath and remind myself that the opinions of strangers aren't worth considering. The people who truly know me are the only ones that matter. And they're right here.

I tried to dress more festive tonight, with a red sweater dress and navy-blue scarf that has pretty white birds on it. They're not eagles, but oh well. I don't have any gear that has Colby's name or jersey number on it, but at least I'm dressed in the team colors.

Mel and Andie walk us through the arena, already knowing the place inside and out. "I love the red dress! Colby will too," Andie says, raising her eyebrows up and down.

Mel makes an excited squeaky sound. "Maybe he'll blow you another kiss tonight!"

Gram giggles at the idea, linking her arm through mine. "Oh, I'd love to see that live!"

We walk through a large door and into the bustling hallways of the arena. Mel waves an arm for us to follow her, then leads us straight through the crowd to our seats. We're in the corner near the Eagles' starting zone, about ten rows up. I'm relieved to be slightly further up from the ice this time, I have a better view from up here.

As expected, there are fans holding signs. Some of them are kids with cute handmade posters. And others are women. I ignore the ones pining for Colby and instead giggle with the girls about one for Bruce that says, *you can guard my net anytime, Brucey!*

Gram chuckles. "If only I was about fifty years younger, I might be a puck bunny too."

Andie snorts a laugh. "Girl, if wanting a man who's in pique physical condition, who makes good money, has a great dental plan, *and* gets you free tickets to things makes you a puck bunny… then I'll happily be one."

"That's a great point, actually," I agree.

Soon the guys are announced, the anthem is sung, and the puck is dropped.

The first five minutes of the game passes without much happening, I wonder if the guys are feeling the pressure after three wins in a row.

"I thought you said there would be fighting?" Gram whispers in my ear.

I swivel my head to stare at her. "You're trouble."

She snickers and the crowd starts chanting, *shoot the puck, shoot the puck!*

My eyes move to the ice in time to see Remy breaking away from the other players, impossibly fast. The crowd is going wild, waiting for him to shoot the puck, and hoping we take an early lead. Remy gets closer to the other team's goalie, going to his left, the goalie moves to the left of the goal, but Remy quickly switches to the right. He shoots the puck high, breezing right past the right side of the goalie's head.

Everyone jumps up from their seats, cheering for Remy. Remy skates one full circle around, making sure to high five all of his teammates on the bench. His celebration is quiet and humble, Remy isn't a show-off. I smile to myself, thinking how different this would be if Colby was the one who scored. I wonder what Colby does after scoring. I know last time he blew me a kiss… but what does he usually do? Maybe he pretends to ride his hockey stick like a horse or something that really shows off for the crowd. He's not that way when it's just the two of us, but he takes his job entertaining fans quite seriously.

The game continues, Mitch gets a penalty for tripping, which Andie insists is a bad call. And the other team scores a goal during their power play.

The game is tied up 1-1 as the second period begins. The guys come out of the gate fast and intense, like they just got a serious pep talk from their coach. West captures the puck from the other team's captain and takes it into the offensive zone, he skates it behind the net, waiting for someone to pass it to. Remy skates in and swiftly catches the puck from West. Colby has put himself in the perfect position near the net, and Remy waits for the right moment to shoot it. When he does, Colby catches the puck with his stick and shoots it right between the goalie's legs. We're all up screaming for Colby and hugging each other in our excitement. I look back at the ice to see what Colby does to celebrate, and wonder if he has some signature dance or something. I'm surprised when he finishes giving high fives to his teammates and comes right over to the glass in front of our section. He removes his mouth guard and gives me that gorgeous grin, then he blows me a kiss and winks.

The crowd goes crazy, even more than they did when he scored the goal. Once again, I find myself up on the giant jumbotron. Being the focus of attention like this isn't something I'm super comfortable with, but gazing at Colby makes me forget the people surrounding us. I blow him a kiss back and he makes a show of catching it in his gloved hand and pressing it to his mouth.

Colby skates back toward the bench to switch out for his break and the game continues. I'm sitting happily in my seat, enjoying time with the girls and Gram—who's enraptured by the game, or maybe the players—when an Eagles player snags my attention. More specifically, the name on the back of a jersey. *Evander*.

I'm not sure how I'm just now noticing, but my stomach sinks. There's no way. Surely, that's a common last name. I'm so stunned that Gram tugs on my sleeve. "Sweetheart, is everything okay?"

I force a smile and nod, but my eyes don't leave the player. For the rest of the second period, I'm rigid in my seat. My back starts to hurt from holding my body straight and tense. When the end of the period finally comes, I'm still zoned in on the player with the Evander jersey. Waiting for him to remove his helmet is excruciating. I only hope that when he finally removes it, it won't be who I think it is and I can finally relax.

But my luck has, apparently, run out. Because as he's walking into the tunnel toward the locker room, he *does* take his helmet off. And even though it's been years, I recognize him instantly. Travis Evander. My college boyfriend who cheated on me. The memories of seeing that video of him with those girls comes flooding back to me, making my skin feel like ice… cold and clammy. I don't care for this man anymore, but the memories of being betrayed by someone who said he loved me, are still strong in my mind.

Andie and Mel have noticed my stillness now too, everyone wanting to know what's wrong. I blink a few times, willing the shock to wear off. "Number 92, that's my ex from college."

Mel's eyebrows shoot up. "No! The one with the hot tub and the girls?"

I nod and she wraps an arm around me. "This is crazy. He got called up from the Eagles' minor league team this summer. But he got a lower body injury right before the season began and had to sit out the first few games."

I take a deep breath, the shock of seeing him wearing off. "I'll be fine, seeing him again was just unexpected."

"That's understandable," Andie says.

Gram nods, placing a hand on my knee. "When someone hurts you, you never forget completely. But you don't have to deal with that loser anymore, everything's okay."

I smile. "So true. And thank goodness for that."

My eyes widen when the reality that Colby and Travis are on the same NHL team hits me. Colby will kill him if he finds out. And Bruce, Remy, West, and Mitch will help him bury the body. He can't find out, he can't know. It will completely ruin the camaraderie and team spirit. "Colby can't find out."

Andie levels me with a serious look. "Noel, there's no way you can keep this from him."

"You should've seen his face when I told him about my ex, he was furious. His eyes did this murderous, twitchy thing."

"This certainly complicates the team dynamic," Mel says, biting her bottom lip as she thinks. "I see why you'd hesitate to tell him, but I think it would be better coming from you. This wouldn't be the first time two teammates were at odds, believe me."

I sigh. "You're probably right. Ugh! I can't believe this is happening." Leaning forward, I bury my face in my hands.

"I'm sorry, sweetie," Gram says, rubbing my back with soothing, circular motions. "We'll take it one step at a time. Would it help if I killed him, so Colby won't have to? I'm old, I'll plead temporary insanity."

My head pops up and when I see the gleam in her eye, I laugh in spite of the horrible situation.

CHAPTER 33
NOEL

THE THIRD PERIOD went by in a haze. I don't remember a thing. But the girls tell me we won 3-2. I follow Andie and Mel, my anxiety about the whole situation eating me up inside. Gram holds my hand as we walk through the crowds and back into the quiet hallway that leads downstairs to the locker room. I want to be excited since this is my first time seeing Colby after a game. I want to focus on hugging him and congratulating him on the win and telling him I loved that he blew me a kiss.

When we arrive at the door to the locker room, we're not the only ones waiting. There are other girlfriends, wives, and family members scattered around. I panic again, knowing I can't get Colby alone to talk to him, I don't even know how to handle this mess.

Mel, who's very familiar with anxiety, pulls me away from Andie and Gram. She takes my hand and guides me into a dark, silent annex around the corner. She pulls me into her arms and whispers, "Take a deep breath."

I do as she says, feeling some of the pressure in my chest subside on an exhale.

"It's going to be okay. Colby is a professional. He's not a hot head. Travis is also a professional. I'm sure neither of them wants drama ruining their season. It's going to be okay," Melanie says in a quiet, steady voice. She pulls back, gripping my shoulders with firm pressure. "Are you hearing me?"

I nod. "Yes, I hear you. You're right. I hate that things were so good, and now this."

"I know. And I'm sorry." She gives me another quick hug. "But we got this."

I blow out another breath. "Okay. Thank you for the pep talk. I needed that."

"You've done the same for me, many times," she says, her eyes filled with love. It makes me miss the days when we were roommates and I got to see her all the time.

The two of us walk back toward the locker room doors, Gram and Andie smile when they see I've calmed down. The door opens and we all perk up, waiting to see who's coming out.

A bunch of guys who seem really young exit the locker room, I'm guessing they're the rookies. Next is two older but handsome men wearing suits, they smile and say hi to Mel as they pass. She tells us it's the coach and the general manager.

All my calm feelings whirl into a fury of anxiety again when Travis comes through the door next. He spots me instantly and gives me a slimy smile. He looks good in his navy, game day suit and his auburn hair combed neatly away from his forehead. He's also put on a good thirty pounds of muscle since college. But it's the twinkle in his green eyes that hasn't changed, a gleam that says, *I'm the most important person in my life.*

"Noel! Baby!" He swaggers up to me. "Colby Knight, huh? Apparently, you have a type."

His words hit me like a slap in the face. If only he knew

how much I resisted Colby, how scared I was to trust another athlete. All because he taught me men can't be trusted. Well, I've learned something new these past few months, some men *can* be trusted. Even if they're hockey players.

I straighten my shoulders and look him in the eye. "Good to see you, Travis."

His eyes dip down my body, a body he once told me didn't have enough curves. His lips spread into a wide smile. "You look amazing. Finally filled out nicely."

Gram steps between us, glaring at him like she's seven feet tall. "Watch what you say, young man. I know where you live."

I have no idea what she's talking about, but Travis looks worried and backs away a step. The locker room door opens, and our guys enter the large hallway along with Bruce and Remy. They're smiling until they notice the tension between myself, Gram, and Travis.

Colby is by my side in two long strides. "What's going on?" He asks Travis.

Travis snickers. "I didn't realize you liked leftovers, Knight."

Colby's eyebrows scrunch together in confusion. "What?"

I clear my throat. "Colby, Travis is my ex from college."

He studies Travis for a moment, and I can see in his eyes when he remembers my college ex cheated on me and broke my heart. His usual relaxed body language changes instantly… he straightens his spine, standing at his full height and looking down at Travis with his eyes narrowed into slits. Colby's dimples are puckered on his face, but not from a smile. I'm not sure I've ever seen someone sneer until now, but he is definitely sneering. I brace myself for them to start punching each other, but Bruce and Mitch are beside Colby in a heartbeat.

"Let's calm down, guys," Bruce says.

Remy steps in, ever the team captain and voice of reason. "I'm sure there's a reasonable explanation?" he asks, glancing between Colby and Travis.

Colby's face is red with anger and his fists are balled tight at his sides. He's using every ounce of self-restraint not to ruin Travis's face right now, so he's not capable of answering Remy.

"Travis is my ex," I offer quietly, trying not to draw any more attention than we already have.

Remy's eyebrows raise slightly. "Okay. Well, everyone has exes, Colby. Even you."

"He cheated on her," Colby says through gritted teeth. "He's an asshole. I knew it from the moment I met him. And he's a dick to the staff."

Travis scoffs. "They couldn't even get me the right glove size. Not my problem." He turns toward me. "And Noel, do you think this man-whore is going to treat you any different than I did? He probably already has half a dozen chicks on the side."

Wow. He really hasn't changed at all. I can't believe I once thought myself in love with this tool.

Colby's nostrils flare, and he snaps, his fist coming up and meeting Travis's jaw with a loud, crunching sound. "I would never treat someone like that. You can keep her name out of your damn mouth."

Travis yelps and brings his hands up to his face, his jaw and mouth bloody and red from the impact of Colby's punch. "What the hell! You're insane!"

Travis growls and lunges toward Colby, but Bruce and Remy catch him by the arms. "That's enough!" Remy raises his voice.

Travis yells over him, "let me at him! I will ruin that stupid, pretty face of yours!"

Colby takes a step toward him, bringing his already-bloody fist up as if to punch Travis again. Mitch grabs his shoulders. "Okay, let's cool it. You're better than this, Colby."

Colby takes a deep breath and closes his eyes. He nods at Mitch and says, "You're right." Then turns to me, his eyes going soft at the sight of me. "Are you okay?"

Opening my mouth to answer, a booming voice rings through the large hallway, and all of our heads snap up to listen. "Colby and Travis. My office now!" The man who I recognize as their coach looks absolutely livid.

Colby reluctantly leaves me, following his coach. And I'm left by the locker room doors, trembling from the rush of the fight.

CHAPTER 34
COLBY

COACH YOUNG SLAMS the door behind us, entrapping myself, our general manager, Tom, and Travis Evander in here with him.

Tom and Coach Young stand behind the desk, and Travis and I stand in front of the desk. I'm too keyed up to sit down in the chair behind me, and I assume Travis feels the same way. Coach mutters an expletive to himself and slams his palms onto his desk. Leveling us with a glare, he says, "Tonight's game went great, we won, everyone was fine. So, what the hell are you two fighting about?"

"Colby is dating my ex from college. My relationship with her," Travis pauses, clearing his throat. "didn't end amicably."

"All this over a girl? I should've known." Coach Young groans. "You two are both under contract with this organization. End of story. I don't care if you're friends outside of work, but when you're on the ice, you are teammates."

Tom steps forward, the tension in his stance tells me he's pissed. Luckily, he's not as hot-tempered as Coach. "If this fight had happened in a more public space, we'd be up all night with the PR team handling the aftermath. It would be smart to remember to act professional and uphold the reputation of this organization."

"Yes, sir," I say.

Travis grunts, seeming inconvenienced by this whole meeting.

"I don't want to have you two in my office over girl drama again. Get your asses out of here and behave like adults," Coach says, then points to the door, dismissing us.

As soon as we're out the door, Travis takes off in the direction of the parking lot. As I walk toward the main hallway where I'm hoping Noel waited for me, I have a minute to cool down. I've never hit anyone outside of a hockey game, and even during games, I'm not a fighter. I'm usually the one encouraging everyone to get along, lightening the mood. But something came over me when that jerk was saying things that I knew would hurt Noel.

I flex my hand; my knuckles are red and sore from punching Travis's face. But I have no regrets. He deserved it. I hate that I have to play nice with this guy and learn to get along with him. Maybe I'll imagine someone else's face whenever I see him from now on.

When I finally enter the main hallway, Noel sees me and comes running to greet me. She throws her arms around my neck and whatever anger that was seething through me, is soothed away by the contact. "I'm so sorry," I whisper.

"Are you okay?" She asks quietly, I can feel her lips against my neck.

"I am now." I pull back so she can see that I'm smiling.

"I waited to say goodbye, but I have to get Gram home. She puts on a brave face, but this is pretty late for her."

Glancing at the clock above the locker room door, I see it's almost eleven. I ignore the feeling of disappointment that she has to head out and we can't talk more about this.

Noel takes in my expression. "I know it's late, but you could come over in an hour. After I've dropped Gram off."

I'm exhausted from the game, but the relief that we don't have to say goodnight yet overpowers it. "Yeah, I'll come over. I don't want to end the evening like this."

"Me either."

———

An hour later, I'm standing at Noel's door dressed down in black joggers, tennis shoes, and a grey long-sleeved Eagles tee. I hear a door creak behind me, and glance over my shoulder. Sure enough, her creepy neighbor is peeking at me through a crack in his door. It's past midnight, why is he even awake?

She needs to find a new apartment.

Better yet, she can live at my house... as my wife. Too soon, Colby, too soon.

Noel opens the door, grabbing my wrist and dragging me inside similar to last time I was here. We stand right inside her apartment and gaze at each other for a moment. It feels like we're both looking at each other with new eyes, like something has changed, something has pivoted. The tension between us feels thicker tonight, the way she's looking at me seems different. She's looking at me like I'm her hero. I could get drunk on that look.

"Hi," I whisper, not knowing what else to say.

"Hey," she whispers back.

She's wearing black, silk, button-down pajamas and her face is free of make-up. The lights in her apartment are off except for a lamp beside her couch where a book is laying open. I wonder if she was reading while she waited for me to arrive. I wish I could be here with her all the time, that we could lay on the couch curled up together, reading our books.

She'd give me commentary on The Fellowship of the Ring right as I was reading it and tell me little tidbits and historical facts about J. R. R. Tolkien. Then I would appreciate the stories even more, because I'd have that memory forever.

Finally, she takes a step away from me into the living room.

"Come on in, let's sit down."

I follow her into the small living room. Her entire apartment could fit inside my kitchen.

She takes a seat on the couch, folding her legs beneath her.

I sit beside her, resting my hand on her thigh, needing to touch her. "So, uh… that was intense."

"I can't apologize enough. Obviously, I haven't kept tabs on Travis, but last I knew he was in the minor leagues. I had no idea he was in the NHL, and I still can't wrap my head around him being your teammate."

"I'd apologize for hitting him… but I'd be lying," I admit, making her laugh.

She stares down at my hand on her thigh and covers it with her own. Her expression is somber, and it makes my heart ache. "What's wrong?"

She shakes her head with a heavy sigh. "It's dumb. I'm probably just tired."

"Tell me anyway," I urge, needing to know her every thought. Wanting her to share everything with me, to be her soft place to land.

She hesitates, mindlessly running her finger over my hand, outlining my fingers and my palm. It makes it hard to think, but I persevere. "Seeing him just brought back many painful memories. The heartbreak of someone you love failing you in such a monstrous way, I'll never forget it. I've moved forward, and I don't care about him anymore, but that hurt is still there. And what I feel for you is so much stronger than what I felt for

Travis. You have the power to obliterate me, Colby. If you hurt me, I don't know how I'd move on."

Her admission is honest and vulnerable. I have to take a few seconds to let it wash over me. I love that she feels this strongly about me, it gives me hope she could feel a fraction of what I feel for her. But I hate that she thinks I could hurt her. Hurting her would obliterate *me*. But how can I make her see that?

"Noel, there's nothing I can say that will make you trust me. I think you have to choose to trust me. But I will earn your trust with my actions, it might take time, but that's okay. I'll prove to you that I would never, ever hurt you the way Travis did."

"But—" she begins and then stops. "What if you get bored with me? You could have anyone. There are more exciting options to be sure. You travel a lot; you'll meet other women."

I angle myself so we're face to face, forcing her to look me in the eyes. "I don't want any other woman. I haven't from the moment I saw you. I want a woman who stands up for what she believes in, who makes even the most stubborn students complete their assignments. A woman who will volunteer to take a little girl she just met to the restroom, so she won't have to go into the men's bathroom with her big brother. A woman who is so intelligent it makes me want to keep learning. I want someone who challenges me, someone who looks past what I do for a living, someone who wants me for more than my bank account. Noel, you're the only one who fits the bill. I'm afraid you're stuck with me."

A watery laugh bubbles out of her and she wraps me in a hug.

We stay like that for a long time, embracing each other. It could be minutes, or hours, not a clue. When I finally look at the time on her oven, I see it's three in the morning. "It's late, I should head home."

I move to get up, but she stops me, reaching out and grabbing my hand. "Stay."

"Noel," I start, but she cuts me off.

"It's practically morning already, Colby. Let's just go to sleep." Her sleepy smile is so soft and so enticing, I can't say no.

"Okay."

CHAPTER 35
NOEL

WAKING up in Colby's arms is the best feeling. I never thought about how divine it would be to sleep next to someone all night and then wake up knowing they'd still be there. Well, half the night in this case. But it was so warm and comfortable. I never want to leave this bed. I can only imagine how much more satisfying this would be if we didn't have clothing on.

I push the thought from my mind, because the hard planes of Colby's muscular body curled around me is almost too tempting. Colby stretches and I can see a queen size bed isn't nearly big enough for him. When he's stretched out his feet go off the bed completely. He wraps an arm around my waist and pulls me into him, spooning me from behind. "Good morning, angel. That was the best four hours of sleep I've ever had."

I sigh contentedly. "Me too." Flipping over to face him, I try to give him a kiss, but he stops me with his hand.

"Do you have a spare toothbrush?"

I laugh, probably spreading my own awful morning breath. "Yes, I keep a pack of them here for Helen. Top drawer of the bathroom."

He slides out of bed and disappears into the hallway where the only bathroom is. It's small, like the rest of my apartment, so he won't have any trouble finding the toothbrushes. He's back after a few minutes and slips back under the covers. "Sleepovers are fun." He's grinning and wiggly and it dawns on me that Colby is a morning person. Because, of course, he's a morning person.

"No dimples until I've had coffee." I cover my eyes with my hands. "They're too bright."

He yanks the covers off me and bounces on the bed. "Get up, sleepyhead. Let's make some coffee only to fill it with sugary creamer."

I groan. This was more fun before he woke up.

By the time I slide my fuzzy slippers on and brush my own teeth, Colby has the coffee brewing. I walk toward him, aiming for a morning kiss, when a knock comes from my door.

"Is it your creepy neighbor?" Colby asks in a hushed whisper.

I slap my palm to my forehead. "No. I wish. It's the girls. I totally forgot they were coming over for tea this morning."

"Tea?" He wrinkles his nose.

"We say tea, but Mel is the only one who drinks tea. But that's beside the point!"

Another knock. This one more impatient. Colby takes in my stunned, wide-eyed expression and moves past me toward the door. He swings it open, and the girls stare up at him in all of his fresh-from-bed glory.

"Um, good morning, Colby," Mel singsongs, her voice comically light. "Funny meeting you here… first thing in the morning."

Andie peeks around Colby to look at me, I'm still stuck to my spot in the kitchen. "Well, well, well, I see you had a *very* good night."

"You girls and your dirty minds." Colby steps aside and lets them in before closing the door. "I came over after the game to talk about what happened and it got so late, Noel was kind enough to let me sleep here."

"How nice of you," Andie teases.

Mel smirks. "Yes, very hospitable."

Colby bites his bottom lip, obviously enjoying this. "Well, the coffee is brewing, I'll leave you to your girl talk." He takes a few long strides until he's standing in front of me, then cups my face in his big, warm hands. He kisses me deeply, not caring that the girls are watching. "I'll see you later, angel."

"Yeah, see you," is all I can manage to squeak out. Colby opens the front door, glancing over his shoulder just long enough to give me that dimpled grin, then leaves with a friendly wave goodbye to the girls.

Chaos ensues the second the door closes, Mel and Andie are jumping and squealing and tugging on my pajamas.

"Wow! Like wow!" Mel giggles. "We want to hear everything."

I roll my eyes and sigh. "There's nothing to tell."

Andie crosses her arms. "You mean to tell me, Colby Knight, sex-god of the NHL, spent the night at your house, and nothing happened besides actual sleeping?"

Grabbing a mug, I pour myself a cup of coffee. "That's exactly what I'm saying. The whole thing with my ex was emotional. We needed to talk it out. He was exhausted from the game, and I was mentally exhausted." A smile tugs at my lips. "But it was *really* nice to wake up to him."

They both go *aww*.

Andie grabs a mug from the cabinet. "How are you doing after the drama last night, are you okay?"

I blow out a breath, leaning my back against the kitchen counter. "Yeah, I'm okay. It drudged up a lot of old heartache.

And I know Colby's past doesn't matter, that's in the past... but trust doesn't come easy for me. And with their travel schedule..." I gulp. "I worry he might hurt me too."

Andie takes a step toward me and places a hand on my shoulder. "Colby is crazy about you and has been into you for over a year, right?"

Mel nods, answering her question.

Andie continues, "But trusting someone takes time, and you guys are just starting out. I think in time, Colby will win your trust."

"Exactly. I agree," Mel says, coming to stand at my other side. "And if he does hurt you, which he won't, I know four guys who would gladly kick his ass."

We laugh at her comment, but there's a heaviness in the pit of my stomach at the thought of Colby hurting me. And the reminder that he *could* crush my heart.

Andie and Mel make their tea and coffee and we move into the living room.

"I think it shows how much he's matured, and how much he likes you, that he's not only here for the physical benefits. He's putting the work in to have a relationship with you. Doing whatever he can just to spend time with you. It's extremely romantic, actually," Mel says, nestling back into the sofa with a dreamy sigh.

Andie sits on the rug across from us, her brown eyes sparkle with unshed tears. "I agree, he's being really sweet." She pauses, her lips pulling up in a smirk. "And I know violence isn't always the answer, but how hot was it when he punched your ex?"

I laugh. "I'm actually relieved you said that, because I felt guilty for internally swooning. I mean, in the moment it was terrifying, my hands wouldn't stop shaking. But afterward I realized how sexy it was. I always thought I needed someone safe, someone like Dexter. A man who was reserved and wouldn't make my heart race. But Dexter would have never punched someone for me, and I didn't know how much I needed a man who was willing to fight for me... literally."

Andie and Mel nod as they listen, obviously agreeing with my thoughts.

"Did I tell you guys Colby is reading The Lord of the Rings trilogy?" I ask, taking a small sip of my coffee.

Andie gasps. "Stop it! That's too cute!"

Mel smiles. "He's kind of perfect for you," she muses. "On paper you two don't make sense, but seeing it in person?" She mimics a chef's kiss with her fingers.

I smile back. "Yeah, I think you're right. He is kind of perfect for me."

CHAPTER 36
COLBY

I HAVEN'T SEEN Noel in a week, and I miss her. Between our game schedules and midterms she has to grade, we've both been slammed. We lost our Sunday afternoon game today; I swear Sunday games are bad luck or something. The team is meeting at a bar tonight for dinner and drinks. We do this every month to build team spirit. This whole week I've been able to ignore freaking Travis Evander. When we're on the ice, I treat him the same as any other player. And off ice, I avoid him completely. But I'm not sure I can avoid him at a team dinner event like this.

And just to make it worse, Noel can't be my date tonight. It's her last night to finalize grades before giving her students their graded papers tomorrow morning. Maybe it's better she doesn't have to see Travis at all, but selfishly, I want her there by my side.

I can't even celebrate with her being done with midterms by going to Pancake Palace, because tomorrow night we leave for a stint of away games in California.

Walking into the swanky bar in downtown Alexandria, I'm grouchy. I'm almost never grouchy. But I want to hang out with my girl, and instead I'm having dinner with a bunch of guys I've seen all week. Not that I don't love them, I just love Noel more. Yep, love. I love her, and I want to tell her that, and also show her a surprise I've been working on… okay, the contractors I hired have been working on. But our schedules are stupid.

Did I mention I'm grouchy?

Quickly, I spot the group of tables in the back reserved for the team and head in that direction. The bar is nice, it has a 1920's vibe, which makes me think of Noel. Because am I ever not thinking about Noel?

Modern bulb lights hang from the ceiling and the bar is mostly glass with gold shelves. Everything in this place is either black, gold, or glass. And they thought this was a good place to bring a bunch of big hockey players?

There's a saying about a bull in a China shop, but they should change it to a hockey player in a China shop.

West, who's already seated, spots me heading toward the tables and waves me over. Mel is next to him, and Bruce is in the seat beside her. Mitch, Andie, her little brother, Noah, and Remy are across from them, and they saved me a seat on the end, because I'm dateless.

I scope out the rest of the room and exhale a sigh of relief when I spot Travis on the opposite side of the room. Two long tables are full of my teammates and their families or dates, and Coach Young and his wife. The whole bar is lively with music and conversation, but it doesn't make me feel any more festive. West notices my expression and dips his chin as if to say, *sorry Noel couldn't come.*

"Hey man!" West slaps my back.

I pull out my chair and take a seat. "Hey, everyone."

"Don't look so sad. It's breaking my heart," Andie says, sticking her bottom lip out.

I wink at her, earning a glare from Mitch. "Don't worry about me. I'll be fine."

"Will you, though?" Bruce asks, placing his elbow on the table and resting his chin in his hand. "You look like a sad puppy."

I scoff, even though I know he's right. "I just need a good burger and a drink, and I'll be fine. You know me." I pat my stomach a few times.

"Ahhh, you need your protein just like my big man," Andie teases, patting Mitch's belly.

He smiles fondly at her and rests his hand over hers. Andie is for sure the only person on the planet who could get away with rubbing Mitch's belly. Actually, I bet he'd roll over and purr like a kitten if she kept doing it. Love is strange.

Her younger brother stares at them in disgust and I give him a commiserating glance, which makes him smirk.

The waitress, a twenty-something brunette, is blushing furiously and looking terrified, comes over to take our orders. I swear her hands are shaking. Bruce flirts with her, probably trying to get her to relax, because she's way younger than his usual type.

It takes a while for her to get everyone's orders, but our drinks come out quickly. My Long Island Iced Tea is delivered with a flamingo straw and West snorts a laugh. "Sorry, when did you turn into a sorority girl?"

"These are delicious! And don't sorority girls stick with Smirnoff Ice?"

"True," he concedes.

Mel reaches across the table and places a hand on my arm. "Noel is a perfectionist at her job. She doesn't leave her house around midterms. Ever. Even when she was in college, she was like this." She smiles sympathetically. "She's crazy about you, and she'll be back to her normal self tomorrow."

I smile back. "Yeah, I know. I hate that our schedules haven't synced at all this week. But we'll figure it out."

Once our food comes out, we dig in. I'm not the only one here who loves food and eats a lot. We're all savages. The ladies stare at us, half in awe and half disgusted.

"Oh, my gosh," Andie says to Bruce. "Slow down. You're not starving."

"Yes. I am," he mumbles back with food in his mouth.

She takes a lady-like bite of her food as if to show him how to eat like a human.

Remy laughs. "Andie, I've been trying to turn these Neanderthals into gentlemen for years. Good luck." He takes a normal sized bite of his burger, always more mature than the rest of us.

"The ladies appreciate a man who can eat," Bruce snaps back.

"Is that right?" Mel asks. "Then why are you dateless?"

We all laugh, except Bruce. He slides a hand through his hair and gives Mel a smoldering stare. "Trust me, girl. I had offers. I just turned them all down."

Mel rolls her eyes, but she's smiling. "We know, Brucey. You're a total catch."

"Plus, haven't you heard that goalies are the best lovers?"

Mitch groans. "Not this again."

"We pay attention to details, and we're *very* limber." He raises his drink in the air for good measure.

"This has yet to be proven," Remy adds. "But I'm sure you're a real tiger in the bedroom, Bruce." He pats Bruce on the shoulder in a patronizing way.

"Yeah," Mitch says sarcastically, "you're just oozing with prowess."

"And raw, animal magnetism," Andie says in a sultry voice.

"Laugh all you want, but deep down, you all know I'm right." Bruce takes another disgustingly large bite, and we all break into laughter at how ridiculous he is.

Remy finishes his food and wipes his face with the cloth napkin. "Well, I hate to skip out early, but my best friend is flying in tonight for a visit. I need to get her from the airport."

"Amber?" I ask, remembering his childhood best friend. She's visited a few times, and she's super cool. Apparently, she has some douchebag boyfriend that Remy hates.

Remy nods.

"Tell her we said hi, man. Haven't seen her in a while."

"Well, she, um, had a baby. So, she's been busy," he says awkwardly.

"Wow, really? With the boyfriend you hate?" I ask, ever a nosy bastard.

"Yep. But they're kind of… rocky at the moment." I try to read Remy's expression as he says it. I've always wondered if he harbored feelings for Amber. She's cute and outgoing. If I remember correctly, her hair was pink last time I saw her; I wonder if it's still a wild color.

"Ah, gotcha. Well, I'm sure I'll see her around the neighborhood." I smile.

Remy says his goodbyes, waving to the large group of his teammates, then leaving.

"You think he has a thing for Amber?" Bruce asks in what he thinks is a hushed whisper, but it's not quiet at all.

West muses, rubbing his hand along his jaw. "I was wondering that too."

Andie chimes in, "He totally does. It was written all over his face."

Mitch slides an arm around the back of her chair. "Stay out of Remy's business."

"Fine," she grumps.

A peppy song starts playing over the speakers and the dance floor across the room lights up for the evening. Mel and Andie gasp and jump up from their seats, forcing their guys up with them. "Come on! The dance floor is open!" Mel squeals.

Bruce gets up too. "I saw a woman at the bar I want to talk to," he admits with a shrug before following the rest of them toward the dance floor.

I glance over at Andie's younger brother, who looks bored out of his mind. "Just me and you, dude."

He rests his chin in his hands and blows out an annoyed breath. "I asked to stay home and play Roblox, but they made me come."

I chuckle. Noah gets his phone out and starts playing games on it, and I finish my food.

Feeling weirdly out of place, I flip my chair around so I can watch my friends dance. I'm watching Andie attempt to make Mitch do the electric slide, when two women on the dance floor spot me. They smile and wave. I look away, not wanting them to think I welcome their attention.

There's only one girl I want attention from. I pull my phone out and shoot a text to her.

COLBY

> Hey, angel. I miss you.

NOEL

> Ugh. I miss you too. Wish I was there! Can't wait to be done grading.

I'm smiling down at my phone, not paying attention to my surroundings, when two bodies drop onto mine, one female form on each knee. My phone slides from my hand and onto the floor. I look up to see the girls from the dance floor, and I'm momentarily stunned. Being a famous athlete, aggressive female attention is something we, unfortunately, are used to dealing with. I immediately stand up and step away from the brunettes, accidentally stepping on, and obliterating, my phone.

"Hey," I smile, trying to smooth things over and not cause a scene. "Would you guys like an autograph?"

One of the women tries to walk closer to me, and I take another step back. She seems offended. "We were hoping you might wanna have some fun tonight."

"Sorry, I'm happily taken," I say, trying to put more distance between us.

The other one chimes in, "Oh, come on. We won't tell."

"Yeah, we know your reputation," the other one winks.

Wow, these gals are persistent. "No," I say seriously. "That was before I met the love of my life. Would you like to hear about her?" I say, throwing them off completely. "She has a doctorate in history. She's freaking smart. It's hot. And she loves books, she has me reading The Lord of the Rings trilogy. Have you heard of it? It's really good, it has elves and trolls, and wizards—"

They stare at me in disgust, then turn their backs and finally leave. I exhale out a sigh of relief. Damn, no means no, people.

CHAPTER 37
NOEL

IT'S NEARLY midnight and I'm finalizing the grade for the very last midterm paper in my pile. I'm happy to report the hockey boys got it together and wrote spectacular research papers. I'll have to thank the guys again for their intervention.

Piling all the graded papers together, I place them in a folder, then check my phone. No more texts from Colby. I really wanted to go with him tonight, even at the risk of having to see Travis again. But this week has been insane. I feel disconnected from Colby, and I hate it. I pad down the hallway to my bedroom, and the sight of my bed fills me with longing. I wish Colby was here to hold me in his arms all night, to reassure me that we're good, and that our schedules won't always keep us apart.

I slip into my pajamas and wash my face in my little bathroom before sliding under my covers. I try to convince myself not to sniff the pillow Colby used last weekend to see if it still smells like him... I do. But I sniff it anyway, and it doesn't smell like Colby. This is my level of obsession, pillow sniffing.

With a heavy sigh, I grab my phone from the nightstand

where it's now charging and shoot off a goodnight text to my man. He might still be out, but he's probably home by now.

NOEL

> Goodnight. Sweet dreams. *heart emoji*

I wait a few minutes and he doesn't respond. Colby usually responds quickly, as if he's waiting anxiously for me to text him. Which I think is super cute. But he must still be out with the team.

I'm setting my alarm for the morning when a text comes through, but it's not from Colby. The name on my screen is one I never thought I'd receive another text from. I open it right away.

TRAVIS

> Told you this would happen.

My eyebrows furrow in confusion. "What?" Then a photo comes through. I tap on it and my heart plummets. I sit upright in bed, studying the photo, trying to make sense of what I'm seeing. It's a photo of Colby at a bar. I'm assuming the one they went to tonight, and he's smiling, with two women sitting on his lap.

I close my eyes and take a deep breath, but my heart is beating so fast, it feels like it might beat right out of my chest. Slowly, I calm my breathing. Colby cares about me, Colby is a good man, Colby is trustworthy. I remind myself of all the facts about this man, things I know to be true. Colby is caring, and good and honorable. Once my heart rate is normalized, I call him. I'm sure he can make sense of this, and everything will be fine.

The phone goes straight to voicemail. "What the hell." My own voice sounds strangled and unfamiliar to me. I call him again. And again. And nothing. Straight to voicemail.

Desperate, I call Mel. She picks up, and it sounds like she's in the car. "Hey, girl!" Her voice is chipper, and it makes my head hurt.

"Hey," I say, sounding breathless.

"What's wrong?" she asks. "Are you okay?"

"I can't get ahold of Colby. Is he still out?"

She whispers something and I hear West whisper something back. "West said he left about ten minutes before we did."

"Oh, okay."

"Noel, what's wrong? Talk to me." The music that was playing in the background, probably from the radio, turns off.

"Travis sent me a photo." My voice cracks. "It's of Colby at the bar with two women."

"Oh sweetie. I'm sorry. It was probably from a long time ago?"

"It was a swanky looking place, with black and gold decor."

She's quiet for a moment. "Okay, that sounds like the bar we were at, but maybe they were getting a photo or something. That happens all the time."

"They were sitting on his lap."

Silence. "There has to be an explanation. He's not answering his phone?"

"No," I choke out.

"I'm coming over," she says. "We're on our way."

"No, it's late. I'll be fine." I make my voice sound as steady as I can. "I'm sure we'll talk tomorrow, and like you said... he'll explain everything, and we'll have a good laugh."

I hope I'm convincing Mel, because I'm not convincing myself.

"I hate that you're upset and I'm not there. I can come

over." West's voice mutters something. "West says it's no big deal for us to drop by."

"It's really fine, I'm going to sleep now. Big day tomorrow. Midterms," I huff a laugh, trying to sound fine.

"Okay," she says, drawing the word out, obviously not convinced. "I'm going to keep my phone on tonight. If you need anything, call me. Don't hesitate. And Noel?"

"Yeah?"

"Don't freak out. Colby will explain this, I'm sure of it."

"You're right. Thanks, I feel better now." I do not feel better.

We say goodnight and end the call.

But do I have a good night? No.

Do I try to call Colby twenty more times? Yes.

———

After a fitful night's sleep, I wake up and put on my big girl panties to go about my day. I perform my scheduled lecture, one of my favorites, about the black plague. Most of my students are thrilled with their grades, only a few failed. The hockey boys see their B's and high five me on their way out of class. That makes me genuinely smile. Once everyone has left, I prepare for the next class, which isn't for another hour.

A knock from the doorway startles me, and Colby is standing there grinning, holding a coffee in his hand as if nothing is wrong. He's wearing a tailored, royal blue suit that brings out his eyes. The guys always dress professionally when they travel, and his flight probably leaves soon.

His face drops as he takes in my bloodshot eyes, and my crumpled expression and rushes toward me. "Hey, what's wrong?" He sets the coffee down on my desk, then his hands come up to cup my face. "Who did this to you?"

A strangled sob escapes my throat. I was up most of the night, fretting that something might be wrong. Or that he went home with those women, and here he is... well rested and perfectly pressed, asking *who did this*. "I called you thirty times."

He drops his hands from my face and wraps me in his arms. It feels so good, comforting and warm. "Angel, I'm fine. I'm right here. My phone got smashed at the bar."

Remembering the photo, I pull away from him, walking to my desk to retrieve my phone. He appears confused and worried as I hold the screen up.

"What the hell," he says. "Noel. This is not what it looks like."

My hand is trembling, and dread fills my stomach. Those are the exact words Travis said when I saw the video of him with those girls all those years ago, but I remember confronting him like it was yesterday. "Okay," I say calmly. "Please explain then."

He swallows, looking nervous, or maybe scared. "We were done eating, and the couples went off to dance and Bruce was flirting with some girl at the bar. I was just watching everyone when these two women waved at me. I looked away so they wouldn't think I was flirting. Then I texted you, and I was smiling at the text. And while I was distracted by the text, these girls came over and sat on my lap. It was entirely unwelcome. Someone must have taken this photo in the split second between me being startled, and then standing up and stepping away from them."

His explanation makes sense. A quick rush of relief washes over me before that sick feeling hits me again. Because I want to trust him, but my head and my heart are telling me two different things. My heart tells me to forgive him, to throw my arms around him. But my head tells me to protect myself, to not give him the power to hurt me. To never put myself in the position to get crushed again.

As I stand there, staring at him and trying to think. Trying to make sense of this, his concerned expression grows frantic.

He pulls his phone out of his back pocket and holds it up, shiny and new. "Look. I already got a new phone first thing this morning. I would've messaged you last night from Facebook or something if I'd known you were worried. I thought you'd be asleep already. Please, Noel. I need you to believe me." His eyes are pleading, and his hands reach out and grasp mine.

I can't speak. My brain is too overwhelmed for words. Colby squeezes my hands, his eyes wide. "Noel, I have to leave soon. I was just stopping to kiss you goodbye and bring you some coffee. Please tell me everything is okay, that we're okay."

"But," I croak out. "I'm *not* okay, Colby."

He pulls one hand away and glances at his fancy, gold wristwatch, then closes his eyes and exhales deeply. "I don't want to leave things like this."

"I think we rushed into this. I think we need some time to cool off and think."

He shakes his head. "No. I don't need time to think."

"Well, I do." I almost flinch when I see the hurt in his eyes. But I can't think clearly. I need a minute to catch my breath.

He looks at his watch again. "Damn it. Noel, I have to go, or I'll miss my flight. If this is going to work between us, you have to trust me. I know it won't always be easy, but we have to trust each other. I'll give you time to think, but when I'm back from this trip, your time is up and we're talking this out."

I nod, feeling wobbly on my own legs. "Okay. Have a safe trip."

He kisses me once on the cheek before striding out of my classroom. And possibly out of my life. Because I need to either make the choice to trust him with my heart... or let him go.

CHAPTER 38
COLBY

I BARELY MAKE the flight in time, earning myself a lecture from Coach Young. I've been getting a lot of those lately.

How I'm going to put aside my emotions and play three games, I have no idea. It feels like my head is detached from the rest of my body; I'm simply going through the motions. I don't even remember the drive here, but I remember trying not to cry. My heart is tight inside my chest, like it's literally breaking. This feeling is horrible, and I hate that this is how Noel was probably feeling all night, worrying about me. All because of a stupid picture. I want to make this right, turn around and run to her. I don't want to travel for six days knowing things are weird between us. And knowing Noel is struggling too. I want to fix it.

When I finally slump down in my seat beside West and across from Remy and Mitch, they're all staring at me.

"Dude, you look like death," Mitch says bluntly.

"Did Noel ever get ahold of you last night?" West angles himself to look at me.

"You knew she was trying to call me?" My voice sounds angry, surprising them all. "Why didn't you say anything?"

"When you left the bar, you were smiling and nothing was amiss. I figured your phone died, and it wasn't a big deal. Sorry, man."

I run a hand through my already tousled hair and tell them about the girls at the bar and the photo. Then about my phone, and how Noel is freaking out and wanting time alone. My heart sinks again just recounting the whole ordeal. I've been fighting for this girl for over a year. I had her for... what, a week? And I already lost her again. But she's about to find out just how stubborn I am, because I'm not giving up that easily.

Remy blows out a long breath. "Okay, it sounds pretty bad. But it's salvageable."

West nods. "Yeah, she'll come around. We all know you'd never do anything to hurt her."

Mitch looks thoughtful. "Wasn't Noah at the table with you? I bet he saw the whole thing. You have an alibi."

"I mean, yeah. But if she can't trust *my* word for it, does it even matter?"

"True," Mitch admits with a sigh.

"I want to know who sent her that photo. It had to be someone at the bar," West says.

We all turn to stare at him with sardonic expressions. "Really?" I say dryly. "You can't guess?"

His eyes widen as he realizes my implication. Because Travis is the only person at that bar besides us that would have her phone number. But all I can do is stay away from him, and hope he gets sent back to the minor leagues by the end of the season. I glance across the aisle and see Travis Evander snoring away, not a care in the world. Obviously not feeling bad at all that he might've ruined the best thing that ever happened to me. I'd confront him, but I don't think I could do it without punching him again. And I definitely don't want to make a public spectacle, which could lead to me getting suspended, or even fined by the NHL. I just have to sit here and deal with it, waiting for karma to land the son of a bitch on his ass. Hopefully sooner rather than later.

The fact that I want to go over there and strangle him must be written across my face, because Remy clears his throat and shoots me a warning look.

"We need a new game plan," Remy says, changing the subject. "You needed the other one to win the girl, now you need one to keep her."

I scoff, not feeling amused by any of this. "There's no game plan to earn someone's trust, unfortunately."

"Yeah," Mitch says, leaning forward. "But you can show her how much she means to you."

"And how much you love her," West adds.

Hunching forward, I cradle my face in my hands. "I do. I love her."

West gives me a manly pat on the back. "I know, man. I know."

Mitch grabs a pad of paper and a pen out of his backpack. He clicks the pen and looks at me. "Alright, so how are you going to show her you love her during this six-day trip?"

With a sigh, I start making a list.

CHAPTER 39
NOEL

IT'S TUESDAY NIGHT, and I'm in Andie's living room with a pina colada in my hand. The guys' game is playing in the background and I'm trying not to pay attention. Yesterday, I managed to defer Mel and Andie's questions. All I wanted was to sit at home by myself and lose myself in a book, anyway. But one day was all they'd give me, threatening me within an inch of my life to come over to Andie's for some girl time. Not really, but they did threaten to give my phone number to my creepy neighbor across the hall.

"Can we please address the elephant in the room already?" Andie says after ten minutes of awkward silence. "What's going on with you and Colby?"

Mel gives me a gentle smile. "Maybe it will help to talk it out."

On a heavy sigh, I explain what happened, then wait for them to speak.

"Have you talked to him at all since then?" Mel asks, referring to my conversation with Colby in my classroom yesterday morning.

"No. But today he had a latte delivered to me every hour

from the coffee shop on campus." It was hard not to give in and call him after the eighth one.

The girls smile at that.

"Let me get this straight, the picture made it look like girls were sitting on his lap?" Andie asks, her voice is calm.

I nod, taking a sip of my drink to keep from crying.

"Pictures can be misleading. Yeah?" she asks.

I shrug a shoulder.

Mel scoots closer to me on the pale-yellow sofa in Andie's living room. "Do you believe what he said about standing up right away?"

I think for a second. "I do. I don't think he'd intentionally hurt me or flirt with other women. But the thing is, this happened after we'd only officially been together for one week. How many more times will I have to deal with this sort of nonsense? I mean, he's a gorgeous professional athlete, it's bound to happen again. And how long will he stay happy with me before he gives in to the temptation?" My words are coming out fast, word vomit, if you will.

"I know you had a terrible experience with Travis. But not all men are like that. Lots of athletes have long and happy marriages and never even entertain the idea of hooking up with another woman. I honestly never worry about West cheating; it doesn't even enter my mind. He has never given me a reason to doubt him," Mel speaks softly, but her expression is serious. "I think you have to give Colby that chance too, without letting your past relationship cloud your judgment. Or you'll never be happy with anyone." She reaches out and squeezes my knee.

Andie nods. "Mel is right, sweetie. I'm sure it's difficult to put your heart out there after being crushed like you were before, but is it fair to Colby if you're always expecting the worst?"

A throat clears from behind us, and we all whip our heads around to look at Noah, Andie's little brother, who's supposed to be in bed. "Sorry, I couldn't help but hear you guys talking. I wanted you to know that Colby was telling the truth. I was sitting right there at the table when those chicks came over to him. He honestly looked annoyed, and then he started rambling about *Lord of the Rings,* it was weird. Thought you should know." He shrugs like he didn't just save the day and trots back upstairs to his room.

"Well, there you have it." Andie smiles. "So, are you going to stay in the past? Or move forward and put your heart out there?"

I sip my pina colada through my straw until it's almost gone. "Sheesh, you two don't hold back."

"We're your best friends, Noel. We're here to pet your hair when you need hair petters and kick your ass when you need ass kickers. And we know you'd do the same for us." Andie shoots me a crooked smile.

"Yeah, you're right. I would." I smile back. "But I might need one more of these." I raise my drink in the air.

"On it!" Andie jumps up from the couch and rushes off to the kitchen.

————

Wednesday when I get home from work, I start my research. I even brought home some books from the University library and have sticky tabs and note cards. This is my own personal research. I want to learn everything I can about how to trust after being betrayed. Because the girls were right, I owe it to Colby, and to myself, to heal and have a healthy relationship. And Colby is the man I want that with. Desperately. Any man

I thought I wanted before pales in comparison to my need for Colby Knight.

The first book I open is titled, *Learning to Trust Your Partner When You Don't Trust Your Instincts.* Long title, but effective.

This one talks mostly about trusting yourself after your instincts have led you astray. And how trusting yourself is a step to trusting a partner. I'm filling out a notecard when someone knocks on my door. I tip-toe toward the door and peer through the peephole, it's a delivery guy holding a bag. Cautiously, I open the door.

The guy quirks a brow and says, "Noel?"

"That's me."

He unceremoniously thrusts the paper bag into my arms and strides down the hallway. I close the door and open the bag. Inside there must be half a dozen containers of food from Pancake Palace. As I open the containers, I see there's a sampling of everything from their buffet.

This man. How could I ever have doubted him?

Freshly motivated, and with a pancake in hand. I get back to my books.

———

Thursday comes with another delivery. This time in the middle of my lecture. The most ostentatious, and fabulous, bouquet of flowers I've ever seen. All in various shades of pink. Pink ranunculus, pink roses, pink berries. It's gorgeous and smells so good. It kills me to wait until the end of class to read the note.

I rip it open the moment my last student leaves.

Giving you space is hard. I miss you. -Colby

. . .

Finally, I give in and text him.

NOEL

I miss you too. Thank you for the flowers.

I'm beyond ready for him to come home and to talk to him about everything. I feel antsy and fidgety. But I know the distance is allowing me to do some important soul-searching, and we'll be better for it in the end.

CHAPTER 40
COLBY

HEADING INTO TONIGHT'S GAME, I should be exhausted from playing San Francisco last night, and then flying from San Fran to Anaheim this morning, but I've never had more energy.

I'm flying high from Noel's text message and feeling hopeful for the first time since I left her crying four mornings ago. She misses me... that has to be a good sign, right?

And right after I got Noel's text, my contractor called and said *the secret project* is done—my name for the project, not his. The secret project is the key to showing Noel how serious I am. How much she means to me, and how I want her in my life forever. No one else.

Just thinking about being back home in two days makes me even faster on the ice than usual. Like if I skate fast enough, I can get to Noel quicker. I've already scored one rebound during this game and had a breakaway. One more goal and it's a hat trick.

We're in the defensive zone, with ten minutes left in the third. Mitch has the puck and passes it to West. West slides it left and then right, but he's surrounded on both sides. He finds me on the other side of the net and smacks the puck in my direction. I skate forward to snatch it, but my skate catches on something, and I fly forward. My chin smacking against the ice, hard. It stings, but I'm fine. Anaheim's defenseman, however, is sent to the sin bin for tripping. Now we have a power play, giving us a one-man advantage. Exactly what I need for my hat trick.

Remy wins the faceoff, sending the puck to me. I can't get a good shot from where I'm at, so I pass it back to Remy. He shoots it but it hits the bar and ricochets off. West snags the puck and hits it against the boards. The puck slides back around behind the net, where I catch it with my stick and sink it into the net before Anaheim's goalie even knows what's happening.

The buzzer sounds and I take my victory lap, high-fiving and celebrating with my teammates.

Remy slaps my helmet. "First hat trick of the season! Well done."

"Thanks, captain." I give him a salute, then I find a camera, staring right at it, and blow a kiss. I'm hoping Noel is watching, and she knows that's for her.

We win the game 4-2. Coach Young tells me to stay on the bench for a post-game interview from the Eagles' sports reporter, Bobbie. They keep different players after each game, and sometimes in between periods.

Once my teammates file out, Bobbie joins me on the bench with his camera crew. He's perfectly coiffed in a light-grey suit and red tie, his brown hair neatly combed to the side, and his dark-rimmed glasses giving him a distinguished look. Jim, our equipment manager, throws me a towel before following the rest of the team back to the locker room. I do a quick wipe down of my sweaty face and hair before Bobbie's crew starts recording.

"Knight, you were on fire during this game. You're always fast, but something was different tonight. Care to tell us what that was? A new training technique?" Bobbie asks, holding the mic closer to my face.

I grin at the camera. "I can tell you exactly what it was, Bobbie. I got a message from my girl today telling me she misses me. So, this hat trick was for her." I stare right into the camera and say, "I miss you too, angel."

Bobbie chuckles. "There you have it Eagles nation. Love is, apparently, the only motivation Colby Knight needs."

CHAPTER 41
NOEL

COLBY FLEW IN LAST NIGHT—MORE like this morning, I guess—around three a.m. I received a delivery from him every single day he was gone. Day one was a latte every hour during my eight-hour work day. Day two was the bouquet. Day three was food from Pancake Palace. Day four was a gift card to a local bookstore. And day five was a set of silk, button-down pajamas like the ones I wore when he stayed the night, except these have the D.C. Eagles logo all over them.

Then yesterday I received a hand-written letter from him. I read it for the hundredth time while I sip on my Saturday morning cup of coffee.

Angel,

I know you need some time to think. And I understand that. I'm sorry you were hurt so badly by someone that it made it difficult for you to believe a man when he says he doesn't want anyone but you. I'll spend the rest of my life making you believe it if I have to. But you're the only woman who's ever made my heart skip a beat or made me think about cleaning up my act. The only woman who's gotten me to read a book, and the only woman I've ever dressed up as Gandalf for. You're the only woman for me, Noel.

Whenever you're ready, come talk to me.
Love,
Colby

Ugh. Between this letter and his comment on camera after his hat trick the other night, I'm overwhelmed by this man. He's too good. Too wonderful. Too patient. I don't deserve him, don't deserve his empathy. I've all but hurled my past relationship troubles onto his shoulders. And he's carrying it with those big, strong muscles of his until I'm ready to let go of it.

I finish my coffee and pace around the kitchen, trying to wait for an appropriate time to go over to Colby's house and tell him what I'm thinking. Glancing at the clock on my stove, I decide eight a.m. is good enough, grab my jacket and leave my apartment.

————

I pull into Colby's massive driveway and suddenly, I'm terrified. What if he changed his mind? What if my past hurts are too much for him, too much of a pain to work through with me? What if he's grouchy I woke him up? My fingers are trembling on the steering wheel.

I force myself out of the vehicle and stand there in the driveway, staring at his front door. A chilly, fall breeze whistles past me and I shiver, regretting my outfit choice of black leggings and a slouchy sweater that does nothing to block the wind.

With a deep breath, I walk to his door and ring the doorbell. My heart is in my throat, I can't breathe as I wait for him to answer. I wait and wait but he doesn't come.

"He must be a deep sleeper," I whisper to myself before ringing it again.

Nothing.

This is when I start to panic. My heart rate, my nerves, my breathing... they're all too fast, too erratic. I've never felt this out-of-control, even when Travis cheated on me. I was hurt, but I never had the thought that I couldn't go on without him. And not once did I desire to fight with him.

But Colby makes me want to fight. I want to fight with him... I want to fight *for* him.

I pound my fist against his stupid, gigantic door. "Open up, Colby!"

I pound again. "I know you're in there!"

Using both of my fists I knock against the door over and over as loud as I can. "Let me in right now, you infuriating man! We have to talk this out, this isn't over! I love you!" Breathless from my own anger, I slump against the door.

"I love you too, angel."

I whirl around to see a grinning Colby, and a horrified Remy, standing right behind me on the path leading up to Colby's door.

"Sorry, I was getting in an early morning workout at Remy's, we heard pounding and came to see what was going on," he explains.

My anger turns to relief, and a strangled sob comes out. Colby steps in and wraps his arms around me, pulling me close to him and burying his face in the crook of my neck.

"I'll, um, leave you guys to it," Remy says awkwardly and rushes back to his own house.

Colby laughs, his mouth hot against the skin under my jaw. Then he places a kiss to my neck and pulls back.

He opens his front door, taking my hand and leading me inside his house. "I have something to show you," he says.

"Wait. I have some things to say, and I need to say them."

"Okay." He gazes at me with those striking blue eyes, his face serious as he prepares to listen.

"I'm sorry I didn't trust you. What happened wasn't your fault, and my own insecurities made me doubt everything. I've been doing some research…" I pause, noting his smile. "And something that would help me to trust you more is open communication and honesty. I know what happened the other night was random, and your phone broke. But I think if I'd heard about it from you, and not from Travis, I would've been more level-headed, and less panicked. In the future, if something happens, just tell me and talk through it with me."

"I can do that. I have nothing to hide from you, Noel. You can have all of my passwords, phone code, whatever you want." He takes a step toward me.

"You don't think I'm crazy?" I ask, looking down at my feet.

He reaches for me, sliding his hands onto my hips. "Of course not. Whether we like it or not, our past is part of us. But we can move forward, together."

I peer up at him, meeting his gaze. "I'd like that."

His lips pull up into a smirk. "Now can I show you my surprise?"

I nod and he leads me through his house and up the stairs. I've never been upstairs, and it doesn't look like he has either. There are a few empty bedrooms and a hallway before we come to a large loft area with high, vaulted ceilings and wood beams. A vintage chandelier hangs at the center of the room, and there's a window seat in front of a huge window. But it's when I take in the walls and inhale the smell of fresh wood and paint that I gasp.

"Is this a library?"

Colby is watching me closely, studying my reaction. "Yes,

this was just wasted space, so I had shelves put in for you. It looked like your apartment was running out of room for your books."

I spin, looking all around the room. The walls are lined with bare shelves, shelves that are just aching to be filled with beautiful books. "There's even a rolling ladder," I say, walking toward the wooden ladder and taking it for a spin. "I've never seen anything so wonderful."

"I thought you could help me fill the shelves." He gestures toward two large, comfy chairs in the center of the room. "And we could read here together."

A tear slides down my face as I realize how much this man truly loves me. All this time, he wasn't flirting to be obnoxious. I think he would do anything just to make me happy. "You *really* like me."

His head falls back, and the library fills with the sound of his laughter. I soak in the deep, husky sound of it, letting it wash over me and fill all the cracks I've felt in his absence. His laughter subsides, and he pulls me to him, encasing me in those big, sexy arms of his. "No... I really *love* you."

"I love you too," I say, my voice sounding strange to my own ears. I've only said those words to one other man, and they feel so different now than they did then. I'm wondering if I even knew what love was before Colby.

He closes his eyes and hums. "It sounds even better when you're not angry."

I laugh, remembering yelling the words when I was banging on his front door. Fisting his still-sweaty t-shirt in my hand, I pull him forward and kiss him. He sighs contentedly and picks me up. My legs wrap around his waist, and he moves us to the ladder and presses me against it as he kisses me. His kisses are desperate, as if he thought he'd never kiss me again, and I kiss him back just as passionately.

When our kisses slow, we're both panting and breathless. I look him in the eyes and ask, "can I really have your phone passcode?"

He wears a confused expression, probably wondering why I'd be thinking about that during our incredible kiss.

"Because I really want to see how much you put on that bookstore gift card."

He huffs a laugh and kisses me again.

CHAPTER 42
COLBY

THE WEEKS FOLLOWING my California trip are pure bliss. Noel and I spend every moment we can together, and she comes over even when I'm gone to use the library. The library that's now filled with books from our local bookstore. I will never forget the look on Noel's face when she saw how much was on that gift card.

Tonight, Remy is hosting a pizza and movie night at his place, Noel pulls into my driveway so we can walk over together. I open my front door and wait there for her. She steps out of her car and my breath catches. We could spend a lifetime together, and my breath would still hitch at the sight of her. She's dressed in black pants that taper in at the ankle, with a light-pink top, and the outfit is pulled together with leather suspenders and a tweed jacket. She also has little suede boots that hit her at the ankle. She makes everything look stunning. I love her unique style.

"Nice vest," she says with a wide grin.

I look down at my argyle vest and dark jeans. She bought me this vest, and I have to admit, I like it. It keeps me warm without being too hot. I'm a big vest-guy now.

She walks up the stone path and gives me a sweet kiss. My phone rings and I groan but pull it out of my pocket. It's my dad. Weird.

"Hello?" I answer, closing the front door and locking it behind me.

"Hey, Colby," my dad's voice sounds more serious than usual.

"Is everything okay? Did something happen to Ruthie?" Panic shoots up my spine.

"No, no. Nothing is wrong. It's just—" He pauses and Noel stares at me in concern. "I've been thinking a lot about what you said to me. And you were right."

"Oh, okay."

He clears his throat. "I wanted you to know I've been putting in more effort with Serenity, and with Ruthie. I want to be a good dad to her, and a good partner to Serenity. I'm sorry I wasn't there for you and your mother. I regret that, but I don't want to live with anymore regrets."

"That's great, Dad. Ruthie and Serenity are amazing, you're lucky."

"I am." I can hear the smile in his voice, and it lightens a heaviness in my heart I hadn't even realized was there. "I wanted you to know your words impacted me. Somehow you grew up and became wiser than your old man."

I smile. "Happy to help."

"You should maybe, you know, come visit soon. Maybe bring Noel with you?"

I meet Noel's gaze and wink at her. "We'd like that, Dad. Thanks."

Dad clears his throat. "Alright, well, talk soon?"

"Talk soon," I agree, and end the call.

Noel and I start walking toward Remy's house, the driveway is already filled with cars.

Noel tugs on my hand. "We'd like what, exactly?"

"My dad is trying to make some changes; what do you think about going to visit them in Virginia soon?"

Her expression softens. "Sounds good to me. Wait, will Serenity be cooking?"

I burst into laughter, and so does she. "We can sneak in our own food, okay?"

"Deal," she agrees.

The sun is setting as we walk hand in hand on the sidewalk of our large cul-de-sac, and I can picture her living here with me. Doing this every day, having children around us riding their bikes. Nothing makes me happier than thinking about forever with this woman.

We head right inside Remy's house without knocking and the party is already going. We're the last ones to arrive. Mitch and Noah are on the large sectional in the living room, distanced from everyone else. Typical. West is leaning against the dining room table with Mel nestled against him, feeding him a bite of pepperoni pizza. Bruce and Remy are in the kitchen, both with a beer in hand, laughing and talking.

"Hey, gang!" I say, announcing our presence. "The party has arrived!"

Bruce and West whoop and clap. Mel leaves West and walks over, hugging me and Noel. Andie does the same.

I grin at Remy. "Look at you, hosting parties! Such a social butterfly these days."

He shrugs. "The house feels remarkably quiet now that Amber went back home. It's nice to have people here."

I nod, reminding myself to ask him later how Amber's visit went.

West clears his throat, and we all turn to stare at him. "Me and Mel have an announcement to make." Mel ambles over to his side, a big grin stretching across her face.

"Oh, my gosh! You're pregnant!" Andie says with a gasp.

"No!" Mel says with a laugh. "We *just* got married."

"We bought a house right down the street, so we're moving to the neighborhood," West says, probably to avoid any weirder guesses.

"Yes!" I say, pumping a fist in the air. "Now me and West can ding-dong ditch Remy."

Remy glares at me. "Absolutely not. Or I'll ban you from my gym."

West brings his hand to his chest. "Wow, that hurts."

Remy's eyes widen and he smiles like he just remembered something. "Oh, hey! Colby, you might be interested in some team news." He smirks, waiting for my reaction.

"Okayyy," I say, drawing out the word. "What is it?"

We all quiet down and wait for him to tell us the news. "Well, I had a meeting with Tom Parker and Coach Young, and we all agreed that Evander's defensive skills were overshadowed by a few of the new rookies we have. So, they made the decision to send him back to the minor leagues and give the rookies more playing time instead."

I pump my fist into the air and yell, "yes!"

Noel sighs in relief next to me and loops her arm through mine. "I'm glad he got sent back before you two got into any more scuffles. I'm fond of that pretty face of yours now, I don't want it messed up."

Leaning in, I press a sloppy kiss to her cheek. "He wouldn't have gotten close enough to mess up my face. Mitch would've beat him up for me before it got that far."

"Damn straight," Mitch growls from his seat on the couch.

We laugh and everyone grabs some pizza and drinks that Remy arranged on his butcher-block island. Food in hand, we make our way into the living room where his large T.V. is mounted on a wall. The pristine, white U-shaped sectional takes up most of the living room, but there's also a giant puff in front of it. Bruce sprawls across the puff, and the rest of us take up the couch. Noel nestles in beside me; we have to sit close since there are so many of us.

I notice there are a few decorative pillows on his couch that I've never seen before. They have a subtle floral pattern on them. "Nice pillows, man. Very quaint."

"Shut up," Remy mutters. "Amber got them. Said my place needed a feminine touch."

"They look great," Noel says, elbowing me in the side and giving me a warning glare.

Remy nods and takes a bite of pizza.

Turning toward my girl, I watch her and can't help but think about how lovely she is for the millionth time. She's so elegant and smart… and she's *mine*. Sometimes it still feels like a dream.

Noel must sense my gaze and turns her head to look at me. One of her blonde curls falls into her eye, and I bring my hand up to brush it away. I allow my thumb to graze the soft skin of her cheek in the process. She closes her eyes like she's savoring my touch.

"Why are you looking at me like that?" Her voice is barely above a whisper.

"Looking at you like what?"

"Like you can't believe I'm here." A sweet smile plays on her lips. Lips that I want to kiss later.

"Because a few months ago, you wouldn't have been. Or if you were here, you wouldn't be next to me. And you'd probably be glaring in my direction."

"Well, I'm here now." She lays her head on my shoulder. "And I'm here to stay."

COLBY

"WELCOME to this year's NHL award ceremony and thank you all for coming!" John Richards, a retired NHL player and our emcee for the evening, says from the stage in the large ballroom. The room is full of NHL players and their friends and family. Luckily, the NHL awards took place in D.C. this year, and our families were already here for our wedding two days ago.

I glance over at my wife and my heart rate speeds up at the sight of her. She's wearing the sexy as hell red dress she had on at the charity auction last year. I wanted to strip it off her before leaving our house, but she said we needed to be punctual and whatever.

She catches me staring and winks at me. Bruce is next to her, then Remy, Mitch and Andie, with West and Mel completing our round table. Noel's parents and Gram, along with Ma and Charlie are at the table to my left. Coach Young, Tom Parker, Dad, Serenity and Ruthie are at the table to my right. My dad glances up and smiles at me, Ruthie is happily sitting on his lap. He stuck to his word about trying harder with Ruthie and Serenity. And I love seeing the smile on my little sister's face when Dad is giving her the attention she craves.

The room erupts in applause, drawing my attention back to the stage. The platform is lined with the various awards and trophies they're giving out tonight, and I still can't believe that one of them is mine.

The awards ceremony begins, and players are called up to the stage, they give a small speech and return to their seats before the next award is announced.

Noel leans over, her lips brushing against my ear as she whispers, "no one wears a suit like you, Colby Knight." She then kisses my earlobe and pulls away.

I turn my head quickly, reaching out and cupping her sweet face and pressing my lips against hers. I kiss my wife, not caring who's watching. But laughter all around the room and the emcee clearing his throat makes me pull away from Noel and glance up. The spotlight is on us, and Noel's beautiful face is bright red.

"Let's try that again, our next award is for Mr. Colby Knight of the D.C. Eagles. Colby, we know you just got married a few days ago, but can you stop kissing your bride for a few minutes to come up here?"

I mouth an apology before standing and waving to the room. Everyone's laughing and clapping. I lean down and kiss Noel on top of the head and we get a few whistles from the crowd.

When I make it to the stage, I'm joined by Tom Parker and Coach Young. John Richards pats my back and holds up a large, polished-wood rectangle, it has a gold plaque on it with my name. "Colby Knight, it's my honor, along with the National Hockey League, to award this year's Gordie Howe Humanitarian Award to you. Your work with the D.C. Children's Hospital, and your generous donation for their expansion project, went above and beyond. Thank you for your work and keep it up."

Applause fills the ballroom as he hands me the award. Coach and Tom stand beside me as a photographer snaps several photos. Taking a step toward the mic, I smile out at the crowd. "I'm truly honored to receive this award and to have the privilege of working with the children's hospital. The kids always make my day, their bravery and strength inspire me to be a better man. I'd like to thank my wife, Noel, for always coming with me to visit the kids. It's even more enjoyable to work there together. And thank you to the D.C. Eagles for allowing us the opportunity to get involved in our community."

Everyone claps and I take my award and head back to my seat. I'm truly humbled and honored, but I feel like this trophy really belongs to the kids at the hospital.

We came so close to winning the Stanley Cup this year, but we lost in the final round. The farthest we've made it since I've been with the Eagles. Knowing I got to marry the love of my life a few weeks after playoffs was what kept me from losing it when we lost that final game. It sucked to lose, but it also motivated us. Seeing how close we came to winning made us confident that we could take it all next year. And we plan to.

The ceremony continues, and afterward there's dancing. I sweep Noel out onto the dance floor and enjoy the feel of her in my arms.

After one dance, I'm ready to take my bride home. We leave for our honeymoon in Capri, Italy in twenty-four hours and I plan to spend most of that in the bedroom. I'm just about to ask Noel if she's ready to leave when I feel a tap on my shoulder. I turn and see Gram grinning up at me.

"May I cut in?" She winks. The minx.

Noel chuckles and pats my chest affectionally. "He's all yours."

A new song starts up from the band and we sway together. She looks intent, like she has something important to say. "Alright, Colby. You wooed her and married her. So, how are you going to keep her happy?"

I smile. "Keep wooing her, of course. And reading her favorite books."

"Good answer." She smirks and we continue dancing.

Noel's parents pass by us on the dance floor, smiling and enjoying themselves. Her dad scoots close enough to say, "glad we got to see you both once more before you left for Italy!"

"Me too! The wedding was absolutely lovely," Mrs. Woodcock says before her husband whisks her away across the dance floor.

Gram clears her throat. "Now that you two are hitched, I need you to know, I want great grandchildren. It's my dying wish." She gazes up at me with what I can only describe as puppy dog eyes.

I'm at a loss for words, but thankfully, Noel came back to save me. "Oh, no you don't Gram! I've heard that line before."

Gram snickers. "Fine, be that way." She kisses Noel's cheek and then mine. "You two have fun on your honeymoon."

"We will," Noel says, giving Gram a big hug. "But right now, I need to get this guy home."

Gram waggles her sparse eyebrows and Noel blushes. I could watch her blush all day.

I wrap an arm around my wife's waist and pull her toward the exit. "Come on, Mrs. Knight. I want to put you to bed."

When we arrive back at my—sorry, our—house, I waste no time. The moment we're inside I press Noel against the door, kissing up the column of her long, slender neck. This is the best part of her having short hair, excellent neck-access.

She giggles and tries to swat me away. "Colby! Let me shower and take these horrible heels off. My feet are killing me."

I take that as permission to pick her up and throw her over my shoulder, carrying her back to our bedroom and tossing her on the bed. She's laughing the whole way. I kneel in front of her and slide her long, red dress up her smooth legs. Taking her ankle in my hand, I kiss the inside of her calf before unbuckling her stiletto and then moving to the next one. As my hands slowly move across her feet and ankles, removing her shoes and then massaging her sore feet, she stops laughing. She's biting her bottom lip and looking at me the way I've always wanted her to. Like she wants me. Like she loves me. Like she'd give anything for me to make her mine.

"That feels so good," she says in a husky voice, her eyes rolling back as she savors my touch.

I smooth my palms from her feet to her thighs and she leans back, resting on her elbows. "I love spoiling you," I tell her, my own voice now raspy with desire.

"Yeah? Lucky for you, I love being spoiled."

Her eyes glimmer in the moonlight that's peeping in through the curtains. "But I want to spoil you too." My wife sits back up. Her soft hands move to my tie and loosen it. She slides my tie off and tosses it across the room. Her fingers move to unbutton my dress shirt, once the buttons are undone, I shrug the shirt off and let it fall to the floor. Noel's hands meet my bare chest, moving down my pectorals and torso before she brings them back up and links them together behind my neck.

"You know what?"

She smiles. "What?"

I gaze into her eyes, brushing a blonde curl from her face. "I would rather share one lifetime with you, than face all the ages of this world alone," I whisper, hitting her with a line from Arwen in Lord of the Rings.

Her jaw drops. "Wow. You really know how to seduce a woman, Colby Knight."

"You're the only one I want to seduce, and the only woman who would be seduced by quoting an elf."

Noel rolls her eyes, trying to hide her smile. "Just kiss me already."

Sitting on the bed beside her, I pull her into my lap, gripping her waist to pull her more tightly against me. "Ask nicely."

She licks her bottom lip. "Kiss me, please."

"Well, since you asked so politely." I smirk, and then bend my head and cover my wife's lips with a kiss.

ALSO BY LEAH BRUNNER

ACKNOWLEDGMENTS

Thank you so much to my amazing, lovely, talented BETA readers! Madi, Katie, Amanda, Meredith, Casey, and Hannah, you guys are the best. Your input helped me refine Colby and Noel's story and make it even more fabulous.

To my ARC readers, thank you for being so excited about this book! The amount of hype you guys have given Flirtation or Face-off has blown me away! Every post, every share, every TikTok... it all makes a huge difference and I can never say thank you enough!

To Kortney, I owe everything to you for responding to my annoying Instagram message years ago. You know, the one where I asked you how to be an author? Thank you. I'm so happy we're friends.

To Christina, my beautiful cover expert. Thank you for looking over every single draft of my cover and helping me decide what to tweak. You make this author journey so fun!

To Julie, thank you for being the sweetest and most encouraging human EVER. I adore you. You're the $hit.

To my husband and children, thank you for being my biggest fans and supporters. Thank you for muddling through summer break with me while I was working hard on book seven! I love you all with my whole heart.

ABOUT THE AUTHOR

Leah is a Kansas native, but currently resides in Ohio with her family. She's a proud military spouse and has moved all over the country (and hopes to move a few more times.)

When she was a child, she dreamt of writing children's books about cats. Even though she ended up writing romance, she's pretty sure her childhood self would still be proud.

instagram.com/leah.brunner.writes
bookbub.com/profile/leah-brunner
tiktok.com/romcomsaremyjam

Made in the USA
Monee, IL
14 September 2023

42574084R00178